EVERYMAN'S LIBRARY

EVERYMAN,
I WILL GO WITH THEE,
AND BE THY GUIDE,
IN THY MOST NEED
TO GO BY THY SIDE

AESCHYLUS

The Oresteia

AGAMEMNON
CHOEPHOROE
EUMENIDES

Translated by George Thomson
with an Introduction by Richard Seaford

E V E R Y M A N ' S   L I B R A R Y

Alfred A. Knopf New York London Toronto

260

THIS IS A BORZOI BOOK

PUBLISHED BY ALFRED A. KNOPF

First included in Everyman's Library, 2004

This translation first published by Cambridge University Press, 1938
The plays of Aeschylus in different translations first published in Everyman's Library, 1906, 1955

Typography by Peter B. Willberg

 Published in the United States by Alfred A. Knopf, a division of Random House, Inc., New York, and simultaneously in Canada by Random House of Canada Limited, Toronto. Distributed by Random House, Inc., New York. Published in the United Kingdom by Everyman's Library, Gloucester Mansions, 140A Shaftesbury Avenue, London WC2H 8HD. Distributed by Random House (UK) Ltd.

US website: www.randomhouse/everymans

ISBN: 1-4000-4192-9 (US)
1-85715-260-3 (UK)

A CIP catalogue reference for this book is available from the British Library

Library of Congress Cataloging-in-Publication Data
Aeschylus
[Oresteia. English & Greek]
The Oresteia / Aeschylus; translated by George Thomson; introduction by Richard Seaford.
p. cm.—(Everyman's library)
Originally published: The Oresteia of Aeschylus. Cambridge [Eng.]: The University Press, 1938.
Includes bibliographical references.
Contents: Agamemnon—Choephoroe—Eumenides.
ISBN 4-4000-4192-9 (alk. paper)
1. Aeschylus—Translations into English. 2. Agamemnon (Greek mythology)—Drama. 3. Orestes (Greek mythology)—Drama. 4. Electra (Greek mythology)—Drama. I. Thomson, George Derwent. II. Aeschylus. Agamemnon. English & Greek. III. Aeschylus. Choephori. English & Greek. IV. Aeschylus. Eumenides. English & Greek. V. Title.

Book design by Barbara de Wilde and Carol Devine Carson

Typeset in the UK by AccComputing, North Barrow, Somerset
Printed and bound in Germany by GGP Media, Pössneck

AESCHYLUS

CONTENTS

INTRODUCTION

Of all that humankind has lost there is no loss more heartbreaking than the dramas of Aeschylus. From the eighty or so that he wrote only six have survived, of astonishing quality (perhaps seven, but it is now believed by many that he did not write the *Prometheus Bound*). But they too could easily have been allowed to perish by the indifference of the early Christian era. The only surviving trilogy is the *Oresteia*, for which we owe much to a few individuals: notably to the scribe who somewhere in the Byzantine east in the tenth century copied most of it into a parchment codex, and to Giovanni Aurispa, who purchased the codex in Constantinople and in 1423 brought it to Italy, where it can now be consulted in the Laurentian library in Florence.

In the next century the young poet Ronsard, on being read the *Prometheus Bound* by his teacher Dorat, exclaimed 'Et quoy, mon maistre, m'avez vous caché, si long temps ces richesses?' Greek tragedy was by now secure, even if still known only to a few enthusiasts. Two centuries later, in Fielding's *Joseph Andrews*, Parson Adams walking on a country road becomes totally absorbed, for three whole miles, in a passage of Aeschylus. When arrested, his Greek text is taken by the rustic authorities to be written in code, and 'Aeschylus' to be a false name for himself. Another country clergyman, Mr Irwine in George Eliot's *Adam Bede* (set at the close of the eighteenth century), dips into Aeschylus at breakfast, and quotes at Arthur Donnithorne the 'unloving love' of *Libation Bearers* 600.

In the late eighteenth and nineteenth centuries the perception of Greek tragedy changed radically, in two respects in particular. Firstly, it began to be understood historically. For centuries after the importation of the manuscripts into western Europe, the study of ancient Greek texts had focused on the attempt to understand the difficulties of language and to remove the various corruptions that had entered the text in the process of transmission from one copy to another, i.e. to restore what the author had written. This process continues even today, not least for the seriously corrupted text of the *Oresteia*. But from early in the nineteenth century, with the development of the historical and social sciences, there began in earnest the attempt to understand Greek culture as a whole. In Britain this approach eventually acquired an influential form in the application of the new subject of anthropology to early Greek texts by the so-called Cambridge School of – among others – Jane Harrison, Gilbert Murray and F. M. Cornford.

Secondly, Greek tragedy became an aesthetic and even a spiritual ideal, and a major source of inspiration for poetic creation – for instance in Shelley's *Prometheus Unbound*. In 1864 Matthew Arnold listed Aeschylus as one of the 'four great names' in his argument that 530–430 BC was a period 'in which poetry made, it seems to me, the noblest, the most successful effort she has ever made as the priestess of the imaginative reason, of the element by which the modern spirit, if it would live right, has chiefly to live', a period which by itself goes far towards establishing Greece as 'a country hardly less important to mankind than Judaea' (*Essays in Criticism*). By the time of the Cambridge School – in the late Victorian and Edwardian era – it had achieved a higher status among more people than at any time since classical antiquity, occupying a pinnacle of the educational system and entering the theatrical repertoire. In 1900 the *Oresteia* was called by Swinburne 'probably on the whole the greatest spiritual work of man' (*Letters* vol. 6).

In Germany these two developments were even more thoroughgoing. A landmark in the historical understanding of the *Oresteia* was Karl Otfried Müller's book (1833) on the third play of the trilogy. With the aim of 'placing the reader in a position to regard the *Eumenides* no longer as the airy production of a strange world view, but as invested with present life and reality', it includes discussion of the cult of the Erinyes (Furies), of the physical appearance of chorus, actors and theatre, and of the historical development of the law court. For Müller the *Oresteia* lent itself to a new kind of project, the combination of various subjects generally pursued separately – poetry, archaeology, religion, political and social history –

arising from the immense ambition to understand the ancient world as a whole.

If the historical approach had been interested in the social conditions for the flowering of Athenian tragedy, then our second development – the aesthetic and spiritual idealization of tragedy – could extend even to an interest in recreating those conditions. Richard Wagner describes his first encounter (1847) with the *Oresteia* as follows.

> I could see the *Oresteia* with my mind's eye as if actually being performed, and its impact on me was indescribable. There was nothing to equal the exalted emotion evoked in me by *Agamemnon*; and to the close of *Eumenides* I remained in a state of transport from which I have never really returned to become fully reconciled with modern literature. My ideas about the significance of drama, and especially of the theatre itself, were decisively moulded by these impressions. (*Mein Leben*)

At this time he was, as Court Kapellmeister at Dresden, hoping to remove opera from the control of the Court by transforming the Court theatre into a National theatre. In 1849 he participated in revolutionary activity in Dresden, and was after its failure exiled from Germany. In the same year he wrote, in his *Art and Revolution*, that

> the deposition of Aeschylus was the first step downwards from the height of Greek tragedy, the beginning of the dissolution of the Athenian state.

Aeschylus had not always been elevated above his tragic successors. In the influential lectures of A. W. Schlegel (1808) pride of place had been given to Sophocles, whose perfect proportion and harmonious sweetness contrast with Aeschylus's terrifying sublimity. The primacy of Aeschylean tragedy for Wagner belongs to his revolutionary politics. The decline of Athenian tragedy was, he believed, also social and political decline. In Athens the whole community had gathered in the theatre to rediscover and understand itself in drama that was not yet subject to the modern divisions between art and religion, between creator, performance and public, and between words, music and dance. Athenian tragedy was performed at a religious festival, the City Dionysia, and contained the most profound religious and philosophical thought. The earliest tragedians directed and acted in their plays, and the shape of the theatre meant that the chorus of citizens 'stood, as it were, at the heart of the audience' (*On Actors and Singers*). The decline of tragedy that accompanied the 'dissolution of the Athenian state' was also *analogous* to it: just as the communal spirit was fragmented into numerous egotisms, so tragedy, according to Wagner, disintegrated into its individual components – rhetoric, painting, music, etc. Accordingly the most perfect realization of a free and self-conscious community is, for Wagner, the *Gesamtkunstwerk*, the total work of art, in which the disintegrated constituents of tragedy are reunited. Whereas Greek art was *conservative*, because it expressed public consciousness, art today exists only in the consciousness of the individual, and so 'with us, true art is *revolutionary*, since its very existence is at odds with the prevailing generality of mankind'.

Later in his life Wagner maintained in conversation with his wife Cosima that the *Oresteia* was 'the most perfect thing in every way, religious, philosophic, poetic, artistic'. Its influence (and that of the *Prometheus Bound*) on his *Ring* cycle can be traced in some detail. Suffice it here to point to the trilogy form (the *Ring* is a 'stage festival-play for three days and a preliminary evening'), and to the reduction – in both *Oresteia* and *Ring* – of an epic profusion of communally created, all-embracing mythology to a single, seemingly inevitable sequence of relatively few scenes, sometimes spectacular but always simple, in which the focus is often on a confrontation between two individuals.

But on the whole the *Oresteia* was for Wagner an inspiration rather than a model to be imitated. For instance, the role of the tragic chorus in expressing the emotion arising from the action had passed, according to Wagner, to the continuous accompaniment provided by the orchestra. Nor could the festival theatre at Bayreuth simply reproduce the theatre of Dionysus at Athens. Wagner's insistence on the social preconditions for great art arose – at least in part – from his perception of the need for political revolution if his own operatic aims were to be realized, and was followed by disappointment and political withdrawal. But it has contributed more to the understanding of Aeschylus than has much professional scholarship.

The idea that in the surviving Greek tragedies we can see a process of degeneration was shared by Wagner with his young friend and fervent admirer Friedrich Nietzsche. But Nietzsche, in his *The Birth of Tragedy* (1872), puts Sophocles on a par with Aeschylus (the degeneration comes with Euripides). And he fails to mention the *Oresteia*. This omission is, we shall see, significant.

Nietzsche regarded tragedy as the highest achievement of the Greeks. It had come into being, he argued, as a synthesis of two opposed principles, the Dionysiac and the Apolline. The Dionysiac, typified by music, is the sphere of *intoxication*, in which individuation collapses and a man rediscovers unity between himself and others, and between himself and nature. The Apolline is the sphere of individuation, limit, form, typified by sculpture and by the beautiful (mere) appearances manifest in *dreams*. On this basis Nietzsche perceived in tragedy a subtle relationship between optimism and pessimism. Dismissing the widespread idea of the Greeks as serenely optimistic, he sees Dionysiac tragedy as affirming life even in its insoluble horror. What truly exists is a primordial oneness that is 'eternally suffering and contradictory' and 'requires for its continuous redemption the rapturous vision and pleasurable illusion'. In a later text he identifies the Dionysiac as 'the will to life rejoicing over its own inexhaustibility even in the very sacrifice of its highest types' (*Twilight of the Idols*). The consolation provided by tragedy is 'metaphysical'. It was Euripides who destroyed tragedy by introducing into it mundane naturalism and intellectual debate – a symptom of the new rationalism expressed by Socrates. This rationalism destroys tragedy because it optimistically believes in the ultimate intelligibility of life, in the solubility of its profoundest problems by reason. This shallow optimism is quite different from the higher optimism of the *Prometheus Bound*, which represents a synthesis of the Dionysiac figure of Prometheus, who 'suffers the primordial contradiction in his own person', with the Apolline concern for cosmic justice.

I have dwelt on Nietzsche because of the seductive influence he still exercises, directly or indirectly, on our understanding of tragedy, and indeed on our intellectual culture generally. For instance, the idea that Athenian tragedy embodies metaphysical pessimism is widespread, albeit often without the tenuous metaphysical consolation that in Nietzsche accompanies it. Nietzsche's omission of the *Oresteia* – despite its immense significance for Wagner, and despite the appearance in it of Apollo himself set against the Dionysiac (*Eumenides* 503) Furies – results from the cosmological and *civic* optimism with which the trilogy concludes. Civic optimism, for Nietzsche, was of the shallow kind associated with the rational, Socratic spirit. His theory privileges rather the culmination in heroic downfall that is characteristic of Sophocles.

In discussing the origins of tragedy in choral performance Nietzsche rejects the idea that the chorus represented the people as against the suffering royal individuals on stage:

> from those purely religious origins [of tragedy] the whole opposition of people and prince, and in general the entire political-social sphere, is excluded. (*Birth of Tragedy* §7)

The object of this criticism is Hegel. Nietzsche's fundamental idea – that the Dionysiac principle combines with its opposite, the Apolline, to form a higher synthesis – represents a dialectical process of Hegelian type. But his privileging of insoluble contradiction inherent in the Dionysiac is also the detachment of tragedy from history. Whereas Marx, in creating historical dialectical materialism, had stripped the Hegelian dialectic of its idealism, of the World Spirit, Nietzsche in *The Birth of Tragedy* goes in the opposite direction, stripping it of historical conflict. To be sure, Nietzsche sees the relationship between the Dionysiac and the Apolline as changing over historical time, but they are nevertheless *metaphysical* principles. Born too late to be drawn into the spirit of the French Revolution, he does not share the youthful Wagner's revolutionary interest in the interdependence of community and true tragedy. His distaste for the 'socio-political sphere' of his own day makes him want to exclude it from Athenian tragedy. And although he owes much to Karl Otfried Müller, notably on the origin of tragedy in Dionysiac cult, *The Birth of Tragedy* implicitly rejects the comprehensive historical understanding of which Müller was a pioneer.

This rejection arose in part from the increasing difficulty of any such comprehensiveness. The independent growth of the various branches of investigation had reached the point at which impatience with scholarly pedanticism would welcome the abstraction – from historical complexity – of charismatic concepts that seem to go straight to the heart of the matter. But if the scholars might be accused of missing the wood for the trees, Nietzsche might be accused of enveloping the wood in metaphysical mist. The fierce criticism of *The Birth of Tragedy* by Nietzsche's historicist contemporary Wilamowitz created a famous controversy, embodying a breach that is still with us – between metaphysical and historical conceptions of tragedy.

Nietzsche has had a wider influence than Wilamowitz, even on the academy. Academic work on ancient texts has participated in the overloading of charismatic concepts and the overspecialized ahistorical textualism (text as the fundamental or even the only knowable reality) that have been prominent in the study of literature generally over the last three decades. On the other hand, the most important recent development for the place of Athenian tragedy in our culture has been the considerable increase, in both quantity and quality, of *performances* of the plays, including several highly successful performances of the *Oresteia* as a whole. And recent years have included a renewed recognition of the importance of the institutions and practices of the Athenian polis (law courts, political institutions, the household, gender relations, relations with 'barbarians', religion and ritual, economic processes, etc.) for the understanding of tragedy.

It is as a participant in the polis that Aeschylus appears in two of the earliest texts in which he is mentioned. There is his epitaph, which inasmuch as it contains no mention of his drama, but only his valour in the battle of Marathon against the Persians (490 BC), is for that reason unlikely to have been a later invention. And Aristophanes' *Frogs* (405 BC) culminates in a contest in poetry between Aeschylus and Euripides in the underworld, in which victory goes to Aeschylus as providing the greater benefit for the polis.

At the opening of this contest Aeschylus prays: 'Demeter, nourisher of my mind, make me worthy of your mysteries.' Aeschylus was born fourteen miles from Athens at Eleusis, the location of the famous Eleusinian mysteries presided over by Demeter. Mystery cult was for its initiands a rehearsal for death, its function the securing of happiness in the next world. Of the numerous and various Greek mystery cults, the Eleusinian cult was unusual in its scale, with the annual initiation, organized by the Athenian polis, of large numbers of men and women. Aeschylus's prayer implies a connection between the Eleusinian mysteries and his poetry. Another of the relatively early mentions of Aeschylus, by Aristotle (384–22 BC), implies that the dramatist divulged secrets of the mysteries. We shall see that he evokes the Eleusinian mysteries in the *Oresteia*.

'All our wishes and burning desires,' wrote Wagner, 'which, in truth, carry us into the future, we seek to make intelligible to the senses by using images from the past in order to give them the form with which the modern present cannot provide them' (*A Communication to my Friends*). Both *Ring* and *Oresteia* produce a new cosmology by adapting ancient myth to a new kind of society, the *Ring* so as to transcend – in the twilight of the gods – the curse of the egotistical power of money (or the monetary power of the ego), the *Oresteia* so as to transcend – in the establishment of polis institutions – the reciprocal violence of a powerful household. But whereas Wagner had to seek for his 'images from the past' in ancient Norse and German mythology little known to his contemporaries, Aeschylus dramatized ancient myths that still lived in the Athenian imagination. Probably they lived in the stories told to children. Certainly they lived in visual art and panhellenic poetry. The *Iliad* and *Odyssey* are the only early epic poems to have survived, but there were many others: notably, the 'Homecomings' would have included the return of Agamemnon from Troy to Argos. And epic poetry seems to have been a source of inspiration for Athenian vase painting (on vase paintings of the *Oresteia* myth see Prag in bibliography below).

Another influence on the *Oresteia* may have been a lost work on the same myth by the sixth-century choral poet Stesichorus.

The first play of *Oresteia*, the *Agamemnon*, enacts the return of Agamemnon from Troy and his murder by his wife Clytemnestra, who thereby usurps the royal power together with her lover Aegisthus. In the second play, the *Libation Bearers* (*Choephoroe*), Agamemnon's son Orestes returns from youthful exile with his companion Pylades, is reunited with his sister Electra, and under instructions from the Delphic Apollo murders both Aegisthus and his mother, only to have to flee from the onset of the avenging female Erinyes (Furies). Finally, in the *Eumenides*, the Erinyes pursue Orestes from Delphi to Athens, where Athena establishes a law court to settle the dispute. It narrowly acquits Orestes, and the Erinyes are reconciled to the verdict by the establishment of their cult at Athens.

In relation to what we know of earlier versions of the story, Aeschylean innovation – or at least emphasis – included Clytemnestra (rather than Aegisthus) carrying out the murder alone, and the ending of the chain of violence through establishment of the Athenian law court on the Areopagus and of the cult of the Erinyes. The prominence of Clytemnestra, in an inversion characteristic of Athenian tragedy, gives the female a male role, before the eventual reassertion of the principle of male superiority in a resolution that is both political and cosmological – the incorporation of the female chthonian deities in a cosmic order ruled by the Olympian Zeus.

The male role of Clytemnestra exemplifies the idea of the *unity of opposites* (in this case of male and female). The idea is barely to be found in Homer. It first becomes important in the post-Homeric texts of the sixth and fifth centuries BC, in particular among the earliest ('Presocratic') philosophers. For instance Aeschylus's contemporary Heracleitus proclaimed that 'god [is] day night, winter summer, war peace, satiety hunger', and 'immortals [are] mortals, mortals immortals, living their death and dying their life'. The idea that the world is pervaded by the unity of opposites is in the oxymora of Heracleitus explicit. (The source of the idea is beyond my present scope. Suffice it to say here that the idea, together with its oxymoronic expression, is found also in the formulae uttered in mystery cult. Heracleitus presents his cosmology as a mystic revelation, and the mystery cult of Dionysus was an important element in the matrix from which tragedy developed at Athens.) In the *Oresteia* it is, I suggest, implicit – at various levels from its oxymoronic style to the shape of the plot. For us an alien idea, it will nevertheless – or rather precisely because it *is* alien – be a useful tool to expose the underlying coherence of this wide-ranging drama.

The first instance of the unity of opposites in the *Oresteia* comes in the oxymoronic attribution to Clytemnestra of a 'woman's male-scheming heart' (*Agamemnon* 11: here and elsewhere I give a literal translation). In controlling the household, and killing her husband with a weapon, she unites in herself the opposites of male and female, as well as of dearest (as wife) and most hostile. How can a wife who has murdered her husband perform the due ritual lament? That would be, say the chorus, a hateful act of good will (*Agamemnon* 1545); and the same oxymoron causes her, in the *Libation Bearers* (41), to send her daughter Electra to pour libations at Agamemnon's tomb. The self-contradictory mission puts Electra in a quandary, which she resolves by *separating the opposites* (145–6) – the good prayer for us (for blessings from the dead) from the bad prayer for them (for harm from the dead).

This need to separate the opposites in a world threatened by their unity is a constant theme of the *Oresteia*, and is the key to many passages, some of them obscure or cumbersome enough to have baffled commentators. I confine myself to a few instances. In their first song the chorus of *Agamemnon* describe the events at Aulis surrounding the departure of the Greeks for Troy ten years earlier. An omen of eagles devouring a pregnant hare is described by the seer Calchas as 'favourable but inauspicious' (149–50). It is favourable because it means the sack of Troy, inauspicious because Artemis, resentful at the eagles, will demand 'the other sacrifice', the sacrifice of Agamemnon's daughter Iphigeneia. The description 'sacrificing the poor trembling hare with offspring before birth' (142) is in the Greek ambiguous, for it could also mean 'sacrificing a trembling, cowering woman, his own child, on behalf of the army'. And so the description unites the opposites, on the one hand the 'sacrifice' of one animal by another in a wild pursuit and on the other the orderly domestic sacrifice by a father of his own daughter.

Faced with this symmetry of reciprocal opposite 'sacrifices' – the latter to be reciprocated (159–62) by yet another 'sacrifice' (of Agamemnon: 1106, 1434) – the chorus break off (170) the narrative to sing a hymn to Zeus. Nothing (not even all things together), they say, is equivalent to Zeus. Even were all things to be put on the scale, they would not be enough to remove the weight from the mind. Only Zeus can do that, as the god who, as in Homer, inclines the fate-deciding scales. Equilibrium in Aeschylus is not a dead metaphor, but an image of the unity of opposites. Only Zeus, who has established the principle of learning through suffering (187), can resolve the dreadful unity of opposites implicit in the omen interpreted by Calchas – or rather Zeus in association with Justice: 'the skills of Calchas are not without fulfilment' (i.e. the cycle of violence will continue), 'but Justice for the sufferers inclines the scales to learning' (261–2).

The sack of Troy, prefigured by the omen, is occurring as the dramatic action begins. Clytemnestra's lengthy description of this event begins with insistence on separating the two kinds of cry (of joy and grief) now heard in Troy, which she illustrates with a cumbersome image of vinegar and oil in the same container (334–7). She continues with a lengthy account of the sufferings of the Trojans, the release from suffering of the Greeks, and the hope that the Greeks may not themselves come to grief (by offending the gods, or because of the sufferings of the dead), and concludes with the wish 'may the good prevail, to be seen not in equilibrium'. Similarly, the Greek herald from Troy will optimistically say of the Trojan war 'the gain prevails, suffering does not outweigh it' (579).

Tragedy unites the opposites. Greek cries of joy combine with Trojan cries of grief. The wedding song that accompanied the arrival of Helen at Troy has to be relearnt as a lament (*Agamemnon* 709–12). Even the song sung by the watchman to keep himself awake turns into a lament (*Agamemnon* 16–18).

The lament for Agamemnon is also, in desiderating revenge, a paean of triumph, and the sobbing of Electra is like laughter (*Libation Bearers* 446). Though Clytemnestra insists that oil and vinegar do not mix, the snake that she suckles in her dream mixes milk with blood, the liquid of the closest intimacy with the blood that her own son will extract from her (*Libation Bearers* 531, 544). Even the cosmological opposites combine: fire and sea, previously enemies, form an alliance to destroy much of the returning Greek fleet (*Agamemnon* 655–7).

But Agamemnon escapes the storm. Rejecting Clytemnestra's invitation to walk on textiles that she has spread on his path to the house, he declares that he should be honoured as a man, not a god, and then emphasizes the distinction he has just made: footmats (for men) are distinct from embroideries (for gods). The last clause has baffled scholars, but must be seen, again, as insistence on separating the unity of opposites that threatens us even in the categorization of textiles. But Agamemnon fails to maintain this separation: he agrees to walk on the embroideries, thereby fatally uniting the opposites of man and god, male and female, Greek and barbarian (*Agamemnon* 909–10), and thereby also fails to separate the just from the wicked (798–800).

With Agamemnon dead, the chorus declare that 'this insult has come in return for insult; they are hard to separate (or judge) ... the clan is stuck fast to destruction' (1560–5). Apollo will tell Orestes to go after those responsible for his father's death '*in the same way*, meaning to kill them in return' (*Libation Bearers* 273), with the result that 'violence clashes with violence, justice with justice ... the suffering is hard to put a stop to' (459–68). If each offence makes inevitable a counter-offence indistinguishable ('hard to separate') from itself, then there is no end to the chain of revenge. The display of a male and a female corpse at the end of the *Libation Bearers* will mirror the same display at the end of *Agamemnon*, and evokes the same ironical reference to their lying together in love (*Agamemnon* 1447–8, *Libation Bearers* 905–6). The indistinguishability of opposed acts of violence makes resolution of conflict impossible. Seen as embodying the unity of opposites, the vendetta can have no end.

Apollo threatens Orestes, if he fails to take revenge, with attacks of Erinyes from the blood of his father (*Libation Bearers* 283). But having taken revenge, Orestes is attacked by the Erinyes of his mother. Perhaps the Erinyes of the father may be thought to be in a sense distinct from those of the mother. But Orestes envisages his matricide as a third drink of unmixed blood for the Erinyes (575–6), implying that the same Erinyes are actively involved in the whole chain of revenge.*

Because it is the indistinguishability of the acts of violence that ensures their perpetuation, the third play brings resolution by distinguishing between them. The judicial decision is a 'separation' (475, 491, 633, 752). Killing Agamemnon and killing Clytemnestra are 'not the same thing' (625).

A crucial precondition for this separation is that the superhuman involvement, which we have seen in the first two plays intensifying the unity of the opposed acts of violence, should be differentiated. Hence early in the *Eumenides* the repeated emphasis that the infernal Erinyes, who in the *Libation Bearers* were aligned with the Olympian Apollo, are separate from – and detested by – the Olympian gods.† Crucial in *Eumenides* is the physical presence of Apollo and of the Erinyes, as it embodies the differentiation of opposed principles that allows the judicial differentiation of the acts of violence. But differentiation is only the necessary first step. Permanent escape from the cycle of violence, from the unity of opposites, requires reconciliation of the opposites in a new order.

The chorus of the *Agamemnon*, in their anxiety as the king enters the house, invoke the idea, found in other ancient texts, that it is damaging to pursue health too far, for 'disease, sharing a party wall, presses upon it' (990–2). An excessive cargo – they continue – causes the ship to founder on a reef. Excessive wealth and famine are remediable, but (aptly for the context) blood once fatally shed cannot be restored. This introduces the idea that what produces unity of the opposites (by destroying the party wall between them) is *excess*. Their

*See also *Agamemnon* 163, 1107, 1189, 1434, 1502, 1568, 1580; *Choephoroe* 402, 648.

†69–73, 185–91, 197, 350–2, 366–7, 388–90.

differentiation is maintained by moderation. The desired state is situated between extremes. This applies to the basic goods of health and wealth as well as – we inevitably feel – to the impending act of revenge. Accordingly the same word 'insatiable', used here of health, describes also the wealth that ends in disaster (1331), the disaster that may spring from good fortune (753), and the reciprocal violence (1105, 1485): things pass, through excess, into their opposite.

The Erinyes will in the *Eumenides* (529–34) spell out the implication of this view when they reject both an ungoverned life and a tyrannized one, declaring that god gave power to every middle (mean). This principle, reiterated by Athena (699–700), prefigures the eventual reconciliation of the Erinyes with the Olympian order, in which they pray for the permanent exclusion of 'insatiable' (977) civil conflict from Athens.

The universal prevalence of the middle or mean is an idea associated with another strand of philosophy, namely Pythagoreanism. In Plato's *Symposium*, for instance, the Pythagoreanizing doctor Eryximachus speaks of concord brought to hostile opposites as a principle in both medicine and music (186–8). And in his Pythagoreanizing ontology in the *Philebus* Plato himself clearly believes that the limit should control the unlimited and 'put an end to the conflict of opposites', notably in health and music (25e–26b).

We have then two models for the relation of opposites to each other. One is exemplified by Heracleitus, and resembles Nietzsche's over-abstract association of the Dionysiac with insoluble contradiction. In this model the opposites form in various ways a unity, in which neither opposite is superior to – or can ultimately prevail over – the other. And so tension or conflict persists. This is the model from which the *Oresteia* is constantly trying to escape. The second model, associated with Pythagoreanism, is of opposites which retain their separate identities but combine to form an ordered whole, in which one opposite may prevail over or control the other. This is the model in which the *Oresteia* finds a solution. Although there was an ancient tradition that Aeschylus was a Pythagorean, we need not suppose the direct influence on him of Pythagoreanism or of Heracleitus. Rather, the similarity of ideas in tragedy and Presocratic philosophy may derive at least in part from their common origin in the developing polis.

The process envisaged in the first model is unlimited both in the sense that there is no limit to prevent the opposites successively annihilating each other and in the sense that the cycle has no end. But the second model implies a limit preventing either opposite from prevailing – a limit like the party wall between health and disease. The unlimits with which the *Oresteia* is most concerned are those of reciprocal violence and the accumulation of wealth. They are related in that the reciprocal violence brought control of the wealth of the royal household.* In the end the Erinyes sing 'rejoice in the individual *limits* to wealth' (997).

Resolution of the conflict depends, we noted, on making a distinction between offence and counter-offence. Was Orestes right to avenge his father by killing his mother? The answer depends on the question which parent he is the more closely related to. The claim that the father is the parent of the child, with the mother as the mere environment for the seed to grow in, is put forward by Apollo with a reference to Athena as born without a mother (661–9), and then endorsed by Athena herself referring to her own motherlessness (738–41).

The casting vote in favour of this principle, and so for the acquittal of Orestes, is given by the founder and president of the court, Athena, who thereby resolves the dangerous equilibrium of the tied vote delivered by the human jury. She is herself a unity of opposites, a motherless female who is probably dressed as a warrior (having just come from the battlefield: 400–08, cf. 292–6), as she is in Homer and frequently in vase painting. For her to announce that she favours the male in 'all things' (740) is female endorsement – and so more acceptable to the Erinyes – of a universal asymmetrical relationship between male and female. These opposites – united from the beginning in Clytemnestra as having a 'woman's male-scheming heart' – are finally differentiated and reconciled, by means of opening them out to polis and cosmos. The victory of Orestes is not – as was his victorious matricide – also its opposite, for it is not,

***Agamemnon* 1574, 1638; *Choephoroe* 300.

Athena stresses, a defeat (for the Erinyes). It is the city of Athens that has won the victory.*

Despite the acquittal, the situation is still in the balance. Athena urges the Erinyes not to bring their anger down (the image is of inclining scales) on the city (889). They are persuaded by the offer of cult in Athens, promise blessings for the community, and are finally escorted in a torchlit procession to their new home under the Acropolis.

And so the trilogy ends, as it had begun, with fire signifying joy. At the beginning of the *Agamemnon* the fire in the darkness, welcomed by the watchman as signifying 'release from sufferings', would have evoked the fire in the darkness that signified permanent release from sufferings in the Eleusinian mystic ritual, from which it has been transmitted to the fire in the darkness that in the Orthodox Easter ritual accompanies enactment of the resurrection. But firelight can be delusive (497) or even destructive (389). And the arrival of Agamemnon will not mean, as the herald thinks it will, 'light in the darkness' (527). In both *Agamemnon* and *Libation Bearers* the promise of permanent salvation turns into its opposite. What the watchman saw is generally translated 'light in the darkness' but could actually mean 'dark light' (21). It is only at the end of the trilogy that this unity of opposites is resolved by the direct association of the torchlight escorting the Erinyes with the permanence of their benevolence to Athens (1030–32). The Eleusinian mysteries are a festival of the Athenian polis, and combine permanent release from suffering for the individual initiates with celebration of the everlasting gift of corn for all humankind. Similarly the permanent release of Orestes from suffering brings to the Athenian polis blessings (the cult of the Erinyes, the law court, alliance with Argos) whose *permanence* is repeatedly emphasized.

The *Oresteia* is set at the intersection between the private and the public (the front of the royal house is the backdrop of the first two plays), and between the invisible and the visible. The Erinyes, an invisibly destructive presence in the first two plays – drunk on human blood, 'hard to send out' of the house

**Choephoroe* 1015, 1021; *Eumenides* 744, 798, 904, 916, 1010.

(*Agamemnon* 1187–89) – become a striking and constant visible presence as chorus of the *Eumenides*. We see them first being aroused from sleep – to resume their pursuit of Orestes – by the dead Clytemnestra, who describes herself as their dream. The invisible dead may appear in drama no less than in dreams. Clytemnestra herself had dreamed that she gave birth to a snake that drew out blood with the milk from her breast. And it was to a snake that Orestes had compared his mother as killer of his eagle father, leaving himself and his sister as starving chicks. But then he declares that he will himself be transformed into a snake, as Clytemnestra's dream bids, to kill his mother. But finally, inept congratulation for having rid Argos of 'two snakes' brings on Orestes the vision of Erinyes 'wreathed with thick-clustering snakes'. The image of Agamemnon as an eagle had occurred also early in the *Agamemnon*, where he and his brother Menelaus, deprived of Helen, are compared to eagles deprived of their young (48–54). And then, with the Greek army gathered at Aulis, there occurred the ambiguous omen of two eagles devouring a pregnant hare.

This repetition of imagery in different contexts, somewhat like the Wagnerian leitmotiv, in the *Oresteia* intensifies the idea of the unity of opposites inherent in the inevitable transition (of Agamemnon and then of Orestes) from victim to aggressor and then again to victim. Further, the metaphor of royal eagles deprived of their young seems more than a metaphor: it creates a divine reaction (*Agamemnon* 55–9), suggesting a shared structure, an interconnectedness, between dislocation in the moral and the natural world. It is this same interconnectedness that gives the Erinyes, as agents of reciprocal violence, the power to blight the crops and spread disease (*Eumenides* 818–20, 834). Dreams, invisible powers, symbols, metaphors, omens do not in Aeschylus belong to entirely separate divisions of reality. The omen of the eagles devouring the hare is also a metaphor of what will happen to Troy, as well as being a reality that arouses the anger of Artemis against Agamemnon. Light in the darkness links Troy to Argos as a chain of beacons (*Agamemnon* 293–328), but in its association with mystic salvation seems to make Agamemnon, 'bringing to you light in darkness' (527), into something dangerously like the god of mystic ritual, and it is only when the metaphor becomes a reality visible to all at the end of the trilogy that it announces salvation that will last. The invisible 'cunning housekeeper, the Wrath that avenges children' (*Agamemnon* 162) feared by Calchas – as he indicates the possibility of the sacrifice of Iphigeneia – seems to pass into visibility in the figure of Clytemnestra, who is surely already silently on stage. Later, standing over the body of Agamemnon, she will identify herself with the ancient avenging demon of the household (1502). But of all the transitions from invisibility the most important is that of the Erinyes (and their snakes), for it exposes the interconnectedness of household, polis and cosmos. It allows the dramaturgically impressive differentiation of the Erinyes from the now equally visible Olympian gods, which in turn allows their reconciliation and torchlit escort to their new home. The civic and cosmic optimism of the *Oresteia* depends on *making visible* the terrifyingly disruptive invisible powers of an interconnected universe. The mythical narrative, older than the polis and philosophical cosmology, becomes in the theatre visible enactment, reinforcing the polis and embodying cosmological abstraction.

What does the *Oresteia* mean to us, in our globally interconnected world? It is the first ever and still the supreme deployment of poetic drama (and – at least originally – of music, dance and spectacle) to create an unforgettable paradigm – no less *effective* than the cult of the Furies that it celebrates – of the transformation of reciprocal violence into universal reconciliation. The acquittal of Orestes is necessary but not sufficient. It is because they feel defeated and humiliated by the new male-dominated order (*Eumenides* 162, 173, 781) that the Erinyes threaten the community with terrorism, and it is because Athena offers them the *honour* of cult (827, 895) that the threat is replaced by the promise of reciprocal joys. Now that our cycles of reciprocal violence have broken out of their enclaves and become global, with no immediate prospect of resolution, the *Oresteia* tells us that the humiliation and attempted annihilation of the enemy will never bring peace. Just as the Athenian polis, within the shocking limitations of its time (the exclusion of women and slaves) offers us the paradigm of a society more democratic than our own, so the *Oresteia*, again within the shocking perspective that subordinates the female to the male, offers us a paradigm of the need to make visible and to honour the defeated old order. Those who construct their moral universe exclusively along the axis of gender are not the only group to be sadly impervious to the *Oresteia*. The rulers of our world could not, had they internalized the *Oresteia*, be pursuing their disastrous strategies of winner-takes-all.

The defeat of the old order in *Eumenides* involves a partial transfer of power from deity to humanity (not entirely unlike the transition from god to hero in Wagner's *Ring*). Athena, asked by Orestes for release from the Erinyes, decides that the issue should be resolved jointly by herself and a body of the best citizens. This body is the council or court of the Areopagus, which Athena founds to ensure eternal security for Athens. When the *Oresteia* was first produced (458 BC), the Areopagus, which had long been a powerful aristocratic council, had recently and controversially been stripped of most of its political powers by democratic reformers, though not of its power to try cases of homicide. And so the treatment of the Areopagus by Aeschylus has frequently been analysed as evidence for the dramatist's political views. Particularly significant, it seems, is the declaration of Athena – apropos of the fear and reverence due to the Areopagus – that the citizens themselves (i.e. as opposed to herself) should not innovate laws, because polluting water with mud does not produce a clear drink (*Eumenides* 696–8). I share the view that this 'innovation' does not refer to the democratic reforms, but rather to 'additional' political powers which according to the democratic reformers had been appropriated by the Areopagus after its foundation. It seems that the reformers claimed to be restoring it to its original state as a homicide court, as founded by Athena. And so her insistence on the respect due to the Areopagus serves the cause – as does the respect she accords to the Erinyes – of civic unity through reconciliation of the defeated party. In Aeschylus we see the interdependence of progressive democracy and conservativism. The permanent political cohesion desired by Aeschylus and his fellow citizens in a period of conflict is projected back into the authoritative era imagined by myth. We are reminded of Wagner's insight that whereas in his own time true art has to be revolutionary, among the Greeks it expressed public consciousness and so was conservative.

Several of the issues I have raised are illustrated by what is perhaps the most opaque passage of the trilogy for a modern reader, and the most problematic for a modern production, the lament that occupies much of the first half of the *Libation Bearers*. It is especially important to visualize it as *Gesamtkunstwerk*, as embodying an unusually expressive synthesis of bodily movement, gesture, poetry, typical themes, and music, all dramatically focused on the tomb of Agamemnon. Aeschylus can for all these elements draw on a powerful popular tradition of collective lamentation, known to us from other surviving texts of laments and from dramatic pictures on Athenian vases of the period. The passage also exemplifies our theme of the pervasive unity of opposites: the dead victim is by means of intense invocation restored in a sense to the living, so as to assist in the triumphant revenge; the chorus, asked earlier to sing a 'paean of the dead' (151), which unites the opposites of lament and triumphant song, desiderate (vainly, as it turns out) their differentiation in the eventual replacement of lamentation by paean on the triumph of Orestes (341–4). Finally, it is no coincidence that the chorus is female. Greek lamentation belonged, and still belongs, more to women than to men. An important phase in the development of the Athenian polis was the introduction of legislation restricting the scope and intensity of female participation in death ritual. Lamentation for a man long after his death and by a large group of women unrelated to him (as the chorus is unrelated to Agamemnon) was in the Athens of Aeschylus illegal. At least part of the motivation for the legislation was the political need to restrain the intensity brought by female lamentation to the private pursuit of the vendetta (and still brought in the twentieth century in the Mani in the southern Peloponnese). The cycle of reciprocal violence, with its threat to the cohesion and so to the survival of the polis, had to be contained not only by the establishment of a generally respected homicide court, such as we do not yet find in the narratives of Homer, but also by limiting the emotion that inspires violent revenge for a victim of murder. And so the arousal of this emotion in Orestes and Electra by the female chorus of the *Libation Bearers* is a historically significant expression of the instability ended, in the *Eumenides*, by the foundation of the homicide court and the incorporation of the Erinyes, female inspirers of revenge, into the male-dominated polis and cosmos.

Finally, a word on the translation. Translators often feel under pressure to reduce meaning to what is already familiar to the reader, thereby eliminating what is most valuable and interesting about texts from a different culture. Productions of Athenian tragedy are especially susceptible to this form of dumbing down. George Thomson's translation combines accuracy and readability with the multi-layered richness of the Greek and the original rhythms of even the choral passages.* It is based on his unsurpassed understanding of the trilogy, and on his own edition of the Greek text, an edition that is superior to the subsequent Oxford Classical Text. Of this superiority I will give a single example, which also shows how decisions by editors can make a real difference. It concerns the problem of who speaks what lines, something that ancient manuscripts did not bother to state. In the *Libation Bearers* Orestes, as he plots the matricide, instructs Electra to make sure that everything within the house is as it should be. She then enters the house, and, after a song by the chorus, emerges with her mother Clytemnestra in response to Orestes (and his friend Pylades), who is pretending to be a Phocian just arrived at the house. He announces the death of Orestes, to which Clytemnestra reacts in silence, while Electra pretends to express her despairing isolation, her loss now of all those dear to her (687–95). When Clytemnestra does speak, it is in chillingly calm control of the situation. She imperiously tells Electra to take in and look after the newcomers, adding that she herself on the other hand (that is in contrast to Electra)

*Thomson's occasional use of caesuras in the English text helps the reader understand the rhythm, which is sometimes unfamiliar and obscure.

does *not* lack people dear to her (meaning Aegisthus). All then enter the house, with Electra in fact escorting those dear to her, and we know that the real contrast will be the reverse of the one expressed by Clytemnestra. But, alas, all recent editions attribute lines 691–9, absurdly, to Clytemnestra, and so too accordingly do all translations and productions. A great moment of theatre is in danger of being expunged by poor editorship.

Richard Seaford

SELECT BIBLIOGRAPHY

BOOKS ON THE *ORESTEIA* OR ON AESCHYLUS

COLLARD, C., *Aeschylus Oresteia*, Oxford: Oxford University Press, 2002. Translation with Introduction and brief commentary.

CONACHER, D. J., *Aeschylus' Oresteia; a Literary Commentary*, Toronto: University of Toronto Press, 1987.

DEFORGE, B., *Eschyle, Poète Cosmique*, Paris: Les Belles Lettres, 1986.

EWANS, M., *Wagner and Aeschylus: the Ring and the Oresteia*, London: Faber and Faber, 1982.

GAGARIN, M., *Aeschylean Drama*, Berkeley and Los Angeles: University of California Press, 1976.

GOLDHILL, S. D., *Aeschylus: The Oresteia*, Cambridge: Cambridge University Press, 1992.

HERINGTON, C. J., *Aeschylus*, New Haven: Yale University Press, 1986.

LEBECK, A., *The Oresteia: a study in language and structure*, Washington: Center for Hellenic Studies, 1971.

LLOYD-JONES, H., *Aeschylus: Oresteia*, London: Duckworth, 1979. Translation with Introduction and brief commentary.

MACINTOSH, F., HALL, E., MICHELAKIS, P. and TAPLIN, O., *Agamemnon in Performance 458 BC–2002 AD*, Oxford: Oxford University Press, 2004.

MOREAU, A., *Eschyle: la violence et le chaos*, Paris: Les Belles Lettres, 1985.

PRAG, A. J. N. W., *The Oresteia: iconographic and narrative traditions*, Warminster: Aris and Phillips, and Chicago: Bolchazy Carducci, 1985 and 1991.

ROSENMEYER, T. G., *The Art of Aeschylus*, Berkeley and Los Angeles: University of California Press, 1982.

SOMMERSTEIN, A. H., *Aeschylean Tragedy*, Bari: Levante Editore, 1996.

TAPLIN, O., *The Stagecraft of Aeschylus: the dramatic use of exits and entrances in Greek tragedy*, Oxford: Oxford University Press, 1977.

THOMSON, G., *Aeschylus and Athens*, London: Lawrence and Wishart, 4th ed. 1973.

WINNINGTON-INGRAM, R. P., *Studies in Aeschylus*, Cambridge: Cambridge University Press, 1983.

GREEK TEXTS WITH INTRODUCTIONS AND COMMENTARIES

BOLLACK, J. and JUDET DE LA COMBE, P. L., *L'Agamemnon d' Eschyle*, Lille: Presses Universitaires de Lille, 1982.

BOWEN, A., *Aeschylus, Choephoroi*, Bristol: Bristol Classical Press, 1986.

DENNISTON, J. D. and PAGE, D. L., *Aeschylus: Agamemnon*, Oxford: Oxford University Press, 1957.

FRAENKEL, E., *Aeschylus: Agamemnon*, 3 vols, Oxford: Oxford University Press, 1950.

GARVIE, A. F., *Aeschylus: Choephori*, Oxford: Oxford University Press, 1986.

PODLECKI, A., *Aeschylus: Eumenides*, Warminster: Aris and Phillips, 1989.

SOMMERSTEIN, A., *Aeschylus: Eumenides*, Cambridge: Cambridge University Press, 1989.

THOMSON, G., *The Oresteia of Aeschylus*, Cambridge: Cambridge University Press, 1938, 2 vols. (this translation is taken from vol. 1) (second edition, Amsterdam: Hakkert/Prague: Academia, 1966).

A good edition of the Greek text is by M. L. West in the Teubner series (2nd ed., 1998). Widely used also is the Oxford Classical Text edited by D. L. Page (1972).

CHRONOLOGY

DATE	AUTHOR'S LIFE	LITERARY CONTEXT
(all dates are BC)		
593–4		
*c.*550		Birth of Pythagoras
525	Aeschylus is born at Eleusis, near Athens, son of Euphorion, a member of the old Athenian nobility.	
*c.*521		
518		Birth of Pindar.
510		
508–7		
*c.*501		
499	Aeschylus first exhibits at the Dionysiac festival.	
*c.*496		Birth of Sophocles.
*c.*495		Birth of the philosopher Empedocles and the Athenian statesman Pericles.
490	Aeschylus fights at the battle of Marathon (where his brother is killed).	
*c.*490		Birth of the sculptor Pheidias.
486		
*c.*485		Birth of Euripides.
484	Wins prize for tragedy in the annual competitions – the first of at least thirteen victories in his lifetime.	Birth of the historian Herodotus.
483		
483–2		
480		
c.480		Death of philosopher Heracleitus.
479		

HISTORICAL EVENTS

The reforms of Solon strengthen the coherence of Athens as a polis.

Death of Amasis of Egypt. Persians conquer Egypt. Darius seizes kingship of Persia.

Cleomenes king of Sparta (to 491): expansion of Spartan power.

Fall of the Pisistratid Tyranny at Athens.
Reforms by Cleisthenes democratize Athens.
Reorganization of the City Dionysia (?).
Ionians revolt from the Persians (to 494).

Battle of Marathon: Athens defeats the invading Persians.

Darius dies: accession of Xerxes.

Themistocles becomes political leader in Athens and initiates a programme of naval expansion to combat threat from Persians.
A rich vein of silver is discovered at Laurion in Attica.
Persian invasion. Spartan force defeated at the pass of Thermopylae.
Athens captured and burned. Greek fleet victorious at battle of Salamis.

Greeks win decisive victory at Plataea. Greek naval victory at Mycale.
Persian threat removed.

DATE	AUTHOR'S LIFE	LITERARY CONTEXT
478		
477	Simonides wins the dithyrambic competition at Athens.	
476	First visit to the court of Hieron I at Syracuse in Sicily.	
*c.*476		Phrynichus's *Phoenician Women* produced.
472	*Persians* is produced. Second visit to Syracuse.	
*c.*471		
469		Birth of Socrates.
468		Sophocles defeats Aeschylus, winning his first victory for tragedy, with *Triptolemus.* Death of Simonides?
467	*Seven Against Thebes* is produced, as part of a trilogy on the myth of Oedipus.	
465		
464		
*c.*463	*Suppliant Women* is produced, as part of a trilogy on the myth of the Danaids.	
463–1		
461–0		
461		
*c.*460		Birth of the physician Hippocrates and the philosopher Democritus.
*c.*459		
458	The *Oresteia* is produced. Third visit to Syracuse, from which he does not return.	
456	Aeschylus dies at Gela in Sicily. His son, Euphorion, also a tragedian, is said to have continued winning victories in the drama festivals with tragedies written by his father but not performed in his lifetime.	

CHRONOLOGY

HISTORICAL EVENTS

Hieron I (478–467) becomes tyrant of Syracuse (first city in Sicily). He was made famous by the Epinician Odes of Pindar and Bacchylides, and both Aeschylus and Simonides spent time at his court.
The Delian Confederacy is founded with Athens at its head.

Themistocles ostracized and retires to Argos.

Greeks under Cimon defeat Persians at Eurymedon (Pamphylia).

Death of Xerxes: accession of Artaxerxes (to 424).
Earthquake in Sparta. Messenian revolt.

The aristocratic council of the Areopagus is stripped of most of its political powers.
Athens makes a thirty-year alliance with Argos.
The democratic reformer Ephialtes is murdered. First Peloponnesian war between Athens and Sparta (to 446).

Athenian expedition to Egypt.

AGAMEMNON

CHARACTERS

CLYTEMNESTRA, Queen of Argos
AGAMEMNON, King of Argos
CASSANDRA, Princess of Troy
AEGISTHUS
A WATCHMAN
A HERALD
CHORUS

AGAMEMNON

(The entrance to the palace of the Atreidae at Argos. Before the door stand sacred images. A watchman is stationed on the roof)

WATCHMAN: I've prayed God to deliver me from evil
Throughout a long year's vigil, couched like a dog
On the roof of the House of Atreus, where I scan
The pageant of Night's starry populace,
And in their midst, illustrious potentates,
The shining constellations that bring men
Summer and winter, as they rise and set.
And still I keep watch for the beacon-sign,
That radiant flame that shall flash out of Troy
The message of her capture. So strong in hope
A woman's heart, whose purpose is a man's.
Night after night, tossed on this restless bed,
With dew bedrenched, by no dreams visited,
Not mine—no sleep, but at my pillow fear
That keeps these eyes from slumber all too sound;
And when I start to sing or hum a tune,
And out of music cull sleep's antidote,
I always weep the state of this great house,
Not in high fettle as it used to be.
But now at last may good news in a flash
Scatter the darkness and deliver us! *(The beacon flashes)*
Hail, lamp of joy, whose gleam turns night to day,
Hail, radiant sign of dances numberless
In Argos for our happy state! Ho there!
I summon Agamemnon's sleeping queen,
To leave her couch and lift the ringing voice
Of gracious alleluias through the house
To celebrate the beacon, if it be true

That Troy is taken, as this blaze portends.
And I will dance the overture myself. *(Dances)*
My master's dice have fallen well, and I
For this night's work shall score a treble six.
Well, come what may, let it be mine to grasp
In this right hand my master's, home again!
The rest is secret: a heavy ox has trod
Across my tongue. These walls, if they had mouths,
Might tell tales all too plainly. I speak to those
Who know, to others—purposely forget.

(He disappears into the palace. A woman's cry of joy is heard within. Enter chorus of old men)

PARODOS

Ten years is it since that plaintiff-at-arms
In the suit against Priam,
Menelaus, with lord Agamemnon his peer,
Twin-sceptred in sovranty ordered of Zeus,
Children of Atreus, strong brace of command,
Did embark with the fleet of a thousand ships
In a battle-array
And set out from the land of the Argives,
With a cry from the heart, with a clamour of war,
Like eagles bereft of their nestlings embowered
On a mountainous height, with a wheel and a whir
As of winged oars beating the waves of the wind,
Wasted the long watch
At the cradle and lost is their labour.
Yet aloft some God, maybe Apollo
Or Pan, or Zeus, giveth ear to the cry
Of the birds that have made
Their abode in the heavens, and lo, he doth send
On the head of the sinner a Fury!

(Clytemnestra comes out of the palace and sacrifices before the sacred images)

Yea, so are the twin children of Atreus
By the mightier Zeus Hospitable sent
Unto Paris, to fight for a woman who knew
Many lovers, with many a knee bowed low
In the dust, spears bent, limbs locked in the sweat
Of the close-knit bridals of battle,
Bringing death to the Greek and the Trojan.
And howe'er it doth fare with them now, ordained
Is the end, unavailing the flesh and the wine
To appease God's fixed indignation.

As for us, in the frailty of age, unenrolled
In the martial array that is gathered and gone,
We are left, with the strength
Of a babe, no more, that doth lean on a staff.
For the youth of the marrow enthroned in the breast
Is at one with its age—
In neither the War-god stands at his post.
Old men, what are they? Fast fading the leaf,
Three-footed they walk, yet frail as a child,
As a dream set afloat in the daylight.

(They see Clytemnestra)

O Queen, O daughter of Tyndareus,
Clytemnestra, declare
What news, what tidings have come to thine ears,
What message hath moved
Thee to offer these prayers at the altars?
O see, at the shrines of our guardian gods,
Of the sky, of the earth,
Of the threshold and market alike—yea, all
Are ablaze with thy gifts of entreaty.
One lamp from another is kindled and soars
High as the heavens,
All charmed into flame by the innocent spell,
Soft-spoken enchantment of incense drawn
From the inmost stores of the palace.

Speak, make known what is lawful to tell;
So heal these cares consuming the heart,
Which now sometimes frown heavy and dark,
Sometimes bright hope from an altar aflame
Gleams forth with a message of comfort.

(Clytemnestra goes out to tend the other altars of the city)

STR. I

FIRST STASIMON

Strong am I yet to declare that sign which sped from the palace
Men in the fulness of power; for yet God-given
Prowess of song doth abide in the breast of the aged:
To sing of two kings
United in spirit and sovranty, marshals of Hellas,
Sped with avenging sword by the warlike
Eagle in ships to the land of the Trojans,
Monarch of birds to the monarchs of men, black-plumed was the first, white-tailed was his fellow—
Before the King's house
They appeared on the side of the spear-hand
Plainly for all to behold them,
Battening both on a hare still big with the burden of offspring,
Cut off before her course was run.
Ailinon, ailinon cry, but may well yet conquer!

ANT. I

Then did the priest as he marked them, two and twain in their temper,
Feasting on hare's flesh, know them, the children of Atreus,
Lords of the host, and he spake in a prophecy saying:
'In time the great quest
Shall plunder the fortress of Priam and the herds of the people,
Teeming flocks at the gates, with a sudden
Judgment of Fate in the dust of destruction.
Only let no jealous eye from above fall blackening, blasting the host as it bridles
The mouth of high Troy. For the merciful Artemis hateth
Those twin hounds of the Father,

Slaying the cowering hare with her young unborn in the belly;
She loathes the eagles' feast of blood.'
Ailinon, ailinon cry, but may well yet conquer!

EP.

'O Goddess, gentle to the weak and helpless suckling of the
raging lion,
Gentle to all young life that is nursed by the beasts of the wild,
so now we beseech thee
Bring what is fair in the sign to a happy
End, what is faulty amend and set upright.
And lo, I cry unto Apollo, Healer,
Let her not visit the fleet
With a contrary wind, with an idle, helpless, stormbound stay,
Driving them on to a feast unlike to the other, unholy,
Builder of inborn strife that doth fear no man. It abides yet,
Terrible wrath that departs not,
Treachery keeping the house, long-memoried,
children-avenging!'
Thus did the prophet declare great blessings mingled
with sorrows
Destined to be, as he saw that sign at the great kings' going.
So in the same strain:
Ailinon, ailinon cry, but may well yet conquer!

STR. 2

Zeus, whoe'er he be, if so it best
Pleaseth him to be addressed,
So shall he be named by me.
All things have I measured, yet
Naught have found save him alone,
Zeus, if a man from a heart heavy-laden with sorrow
Care would truly cast aside.

ANT. 2

Long since lived a master of the world,
Puffed with martial pride, of whom

None shall tell, his day is done;
Yea, and he who followed him
Met his master and is gone.
Zeus the victorious, praise him and gladly acclaim him;
Perfect wisdom shalt thou find.

STR. 3

He to wisdom leadeth man,
He hath stablished firm the law,
Man shall learn by suffering.
When deep slumber falls, remembered sins
Chafe the sore heart with fresh pain, and no
Welcome wisdom meets within.
Harsh the grace dispensed by powers immortal
On the awful bench enthroned.

ANT. 3

Even so the elder prince,
Marshal of the ships of Greece,
Never thought to doubt a priest;
Nay, his heart with swaying fortune swayed.
Harbour-locked, hunger-pinched, hard-oppressed,
Still the host of Hellas lay
Facing Chalcis, where the never-tiring
Tides of Aulis ebb and flow.

STR. 4

And still the storm blew from out the cold north,
With moorings wind-swept and hungry crews pent
In idle ships,
With tackling unspared and rotting timbers,
Till Time's insistent, slow erosion
Had all but stripped bare the bloom of Greek manhood.
And then was found but one
Charm to allay the tempest—never a blast so bitter—
Cried in a loud voice by the priest, 'Artemis!' whereat the Atreidae were afraid, each with his staff smiting the earth and weeping.

ANT. 4

And then the King spake, the elder, saying:
'A bitter thing surely not to hearken,
And bitter too
To slay my own child, my royal jewel,
With unclean hands before the altar
Myself, her father, | to spill a girl's pure blood.
Whate'er the choice, 'tis ill.
How shall I fail my thousand ships and desert my comrades?
So shall the storm cease, and the host eager for war crieth for
that virginal blood righteously! So pray for a happy issue!'

STR. 5

And when he bowed down beneath the harness
Of dire compulsion, his spirit veering
With sudden sacrilegious change,
Regardless, reckless, he turned to foul sin.
For man is made bold with base-contriving
Impetuous madness, prime seed of much grief.
And so then he slew his own child
For a war to win a woman
And to speed the storm-bound ships from the shore to battle.

ANT. 5

She cried aloud 'Father!', yet they heard not;
A maiden scarce flowered, yet they cared not,
The lords who gave the word for war.
Her father prayed, then he bade his servants
To seize her, where wrapt in robe and drooping
She lay, and lift her up, like a young kid,
With bold heart above the altar,
And her lovely lips to bridle
That they might not cry out, cursing the House of Atreus,

STR. 6

With gags, her mouth sealed in mute violence.
And then she let fall her cloak of saffron,

And glanced at each face around her
With eyes that dumbly craved compassion;
And like a picture | she would but could not speak;
For oft aforetime at home
Her father's guests, after they had feasted,
Their cups replenished, had sat while with sweet voice she sang
The hymn of thanksgiving, pure and spotless,
Standing beside her father.

ANT. 6

The end I saw not. It shall not be told.
The arts of Calchas were well accomplished.
But Justice leads man to wisdom
By suffering. Until the morrow
Appeareth, vex not thy heart; for vain it were
To weep before sorrow come.
It shall be soon known as clear as daybreak.
And so may all this at last end in good news, for which
The Queen doth pray, next of kin and single
Stay of the land of Argos.

(Clytemnestra appears at the door of the palace)

All honour, Clytemnestra, unto thee!
For meet it is, while our great master's throne
Stands empty, to pay homage to his queen.
What means this glad expectant sacrifice?
Is it good news? Pray speak! I long to hear.

CLYTEMNESTRA: Good news! So charged, as the old proverb says,
May Morning rise out of the womb of Night!
'Tis yours to hear of joy surpassing hope.
My news is this: the Greeks have taken Troy.

CHORUS: What? No! I cannot grasp it, incredible!

CLYTEMNESTRA: The Greeks hold Troy. Is that not plain enough?

CHORUS: Joy steals upon me, such joy as calls forth tears.

CLYTEMNESTRA: Indeed your looks betray your loyalty.

CHORUS: What is the proof? Have you no evidence?

CLYTEMNESTRA: Of course I have—unless the Gods have cheated.

CHORUS: You have given ear to some beguiling dream?

CLYTEMNESTRA: I would not scream the fancies of my sleep.

CHORUS: Rumours have wings—on these your heart has fed.

CLYTEMNESTRA: You mock my wits as though I were a girl.

CHORUS: But when? How long is it since the city fell?

CLYTEMNESTRA: The night that gave birth to this dawning day.

CHORUS: What messenger could bring the news so fast?

CLYTEMNESTRA: The God of Fire from Ida sent forth light,
And beacon from beacon brought the trail of flame
To me. From Ida first to Hermes' cliff
On Lemnos, and from thence a third great lamp
Was flashed to Athos, lofty mount of Zeus;
Up, up it soared, and lured the dancing shoals
To skim the waves in rapture at the light;
A golden courier, like the sun, it sped
Post-haste its message to Macistus' rock,
Which vigilant and impatient bore it on
Across Euripus, till the flaming sign
Was marked by watchers on Messapium,
Who swift to answer kindled high the blaze
Of withered heath, whence with new strength the light
Undarkened yet rose like the radiant moon
Across the valley of Asopus, still
Relayed in glory, to Cithaeron's heights.
Onward it sped, not slow the sentinels

But burning more than was commanded them,
Till at one leap across Gorgopis' lake
To the peak of Aegiplanctus it passed the word
To burn and burn, and they unsparing flung
A flaming comet to the cape that looks
Over the gulf Saronian. Suddenly
It swooped, and pounced upon the Spider's Crag,
Next neighbour of this city, whence at last
It found its mark upon the roof of Atreus,
That beacon fathered by the fires of Ida.
Such were the stages of this torch-relay,
One from another snatching up the light,
And the last to run is victor in the race.
That is my evidence, the token which
My lord has signalled out of Troy to me.

CHORUS: Lady, I will address the Gods anon,
But now with all my heart I long to hear
That tale again and take my fill of wonder.

CLYTEMNESTRA: To-day the Greeks hold Troy; and I divine
That city rings with ill-assorted cries.
If oil and vinegar were to be poured
Into one vessel, you would not call them friends.
Even so the conquered and their conquerors,
Two voices have they for their fortunes twain.
For those, prostrate over their fallen kin,
Brother by brother, old men beside their sons,
Lament with lips no longer free the fate
Of those they loved most dearly; while again
These others, spent after the restless night
Of battle-rout, troop hungry to what meal
The town affords, undrilled, unbilleted,
But seizing each what luck apportions them.
Already in those captive Trojan homes
They take their lodging, free from the frosty sky,
From heaven's dew delivered—O how blest

Their sleep shall be, off guard the whole night long!
And if they honour the presiding Gods
And altars of the plundered territory,
Then those despoilers shall not be despoiled.
Only let no desire afflict the host
To lay rapacious hands on sanctities.
The homeward journey lies before them yet,
The last lap of the race is still to run.
And if they came guiltless before the Gods,
The grievance of the dead might then become
Fair-spoken—barring sudden accident.
Such is the message brought you by a woman.
May good prevail, inclined decisively!
Blessings abound, and I would reap their fruit.

CHORUS: Woman, your gracious words are like a man's,
Most wise in judgment. I accept the sign
And now once more turn to address the Gods.
Long labour has been well repaid in joy.
(Clytemnestra retires into the palace)

SECOND STASIMON

O Zeus Almighty, O bountiful Night,
Housekeeper of heaven's embroidery, thou
Hast entangled the towers of the city of Troy
In a fine-spun net, which none could escape,
Not a man nor a child, nay all are entrapped
In the far-flung coils of destruction.
Great Zeus the Hospitable, him do I praise,
Who hath punished at last the transgressor; for long
Was his bow outstretched with unerring intent,
That the shaft might not fall short nor escape
Far out in the starry expanses.

STR. I

By Zeus struck down. 'Tis truly spoken,
With each step clear and plain to track out.

He willed, his will was done. It was declared once
That God regards not the man who hath trod
Beneath his feet holy sanctities. An unrighteous thought;
For lo, swift ruin worketh sure judgment on hearts
With pride puffed up and high presumption,
On all stored wealth that overpasseth
The bound of due measure. Far best to live
Free of want and griefless, rich in the gift of wisdom.
Help is there none for him who,
Glutted with gold, in wanton
Pride from his sight has kicked the great
Altar of watchful Justice.

ANT. I

As fell Temptation drives him onward,
The dread fore-scheming child of Ruin,
What cure avails to heal? Behold, not darkly
His curse doth shine forth, a bright, baleful light.
And like to false bronze betrayed by touch of
sure-testing stone,
His hue turns black and shows the truth time-tried; he seems
A fond child chasing birds that take wing;
And one crime brands a mighty city.
He prays to deaf heaven, none hears his cry;
Justice drags him down to death for his wicked converse.
Thus did the sinner Paris
Come to the House of Atreus,
Leaving the table spread for him
Shamed with theft of a woman.

STR. 2

She left her own people shields massed for war,
And densely-thronged spears, a fleet manned and launched
for battle;
She brought to Troy in lieu of dowry death.
On light foot through the gates she tripped—
A sin of sins! And long did they lament,

The seers, the King's prophets, saying darkly:
'Alas, the sad house and they that rule therein,
Alas, the bed tracked with print of love that fled!
Behold, in silence, | unhonoured, | without reproach,
They sit upon the ground and weep.
Beyond the sea lies their love,
Here a wraith seems to rule the palace.'
  Shapely the grace of statues,
  Yet doth her lord abhor them;
  Love is there none in lifeless eyes,
  Aphrodite has vanished.

ANT. 2
Delusive dream-shapes that float through the night
Beguile and bring him | delight sweet but unsubstantial;
For idly, even while he seems to see,
The arms clasp empty air, and soon
The passing vision turns and glides away
On silent wing down the paths of slumber.
At home the hearth lies in sorrow such as this,
And more; in each house throughout the land of Greece
That sent its dearest to make war beyond the sea,
The brave heart is called to school itself
In slow endurance | against
Griefs that strike deep into the bosom:
  Those that were sent away they
  Knew, but now they receive back
  Not the faces they longed to see,
  Only a heap of ashes.

STR. 3
The God of War holds the twin scales of strife,
Cruel gold-changer merchandising men,
Embarking homeward from Troy a heap of dust fire-refined,
Making up its weight in grief,
Shapely vessels laden each
With the ashes of a friend.

They mourn and praise them, saying, '*He*
Was practised well in feats of war,
And *he*, who died a noble death—
All to avenge another man's wife.'
It is muttered in a whisper,
And it spreads with growling envy of the sons of Atreus.
They lie still, the possessors
Each of a strip of Trojan
Soil, but the land that hides their fair
Limbs is a foe and foreign.

ANT. 3

A people's wrath voiced abroad bringeth grave
Danger, no less than public curse pronounced.
It still abideth for me, | a hidden fear wrapped in night.
Watchful are the Gods of all
Hands with slaughter stained. The black
Furies wait, and when a man
Has grown by luck, not justice, great,
With sudden overturn of chance
They wear him to a shade, and, cast
Down to perdition, who shall save him?
In excess of fame is danger.
With a jealous eye the Lord Zeus in a flash shall smite him.
Mine be the life unenvied,
Neither to plunder cities
Nor myself a prisoner bow
Down to the will of others.

—The tale of glad news afire
Throughout the town spreads its fleet
Rumour; yet if this be true,
Who knows? It is perhaps a trick played by God.
—Who is so childish or so maimed of wit
To let a mere fiery word
Inflame the heart, then with swiftly-changed import
Flicker out and fade to nought?

—A woman's heart ever thus
Accepteth joy ere the joy is brought to light.
—Too credulous a woman's longing flies
And spreading swiftly, swiftly dies,
An idle word noised abroad on woman's lips.

Soon shall we know what means this fleet exchange
Of lights relayed and beacon-messages—
Whether 'tis true, or like a dream it dawns,
This joyful daybreak, to beguile the mind.
Here is a herald running from the shore.
He wears a garland, and the thirsty dust,
Mire's brother and companion, testifies
That he shall not be dumb nor speak his news
With mountain pinewood flashing smoke and flame,
But either he shall bid us greater joy,
Or else—no, I abjure the contrary.
Glad shone the light, and gladly be it crowned!
Whoever prays that it be otherwise,
His be the harvest of his own offence!

(Enter a Herald)

HERALD: Joy, land of Argos, joy to my father's soil!
After ten years this dawn has brought me home.
Many the broken hopes, but this has held.
Little I thought here in this Argive earth
To die and in dear hands be laid to rest.
O Land, I bid thee joy, and thee, O Sun,
And Zeus the Highest, and the Pythian King,
Bending no more at us his bitter shafts—
Thy wrath beside Scamander was enough,
And now defend us, Saviour, Healer too,
Our Lord Apollo! All the public Gods
I greet, and most that messenger beloved,
My patron Hermes, to all heralds dear;
And those heroic dead who sent us forth,
Prepare to welcome those whom war has spared!

Hail, royal palace, roof most dear to me,
And holy shrines, whose faces catch the sun,
Now, as of old, with radiance in your eyes
Greet worthily your lord who comes at last
Bringing at night a lamp to lighten you
And all here present, Agamemnon, King.
O welcome gladly, for it is right and meet,
Him who with mattock of just-dealing Zeus
Has levelled Troy and laid her valleys waste
And all her seed uprooted from the earth.
Such is the yoke he set on her proud neck,
Great son of Atreus, master, sovran, blest,
Most worthy to be honoured over all
Men of his day. For Paris and his Troy
No longer boast to have suffered less than done.
Of rape convicted and of brigandage,
He lost his booty and in utter ruin
Brought down the ancient mansion of his sires.
The sons of Priam paid double for their sin.

CHORUS: Hail, Herald from the host, I bid you joy!

HERALD: 'Tis mine. Come, death! O God, I am content!

CHORUS: Love for your fatherland has worn you out.

HERALD: So much that joy has filled my eyes with tears.

CHORUS: Then bitterness was not unmixed with sweet.

HERALD: Sweetness? How so? Your wit eludes me there.

CHORUS: You loved in absence those who loved again.

HERALD: The country yearned for us, who yearned for her?

CHORUS: Even so, with many a groan of dark surmise.

HERALD: Whence came this sullen misgiving for our sake?

CHORUS: Let silence heal—I learnt that long ago.

HERALD: How? In our absence had you cause to fear?

CHORUS: As you have said, now it were joy to die.

HERALD: Yes, for the end is well. Our enterprise
At last is well concluded, though in part
The issue be found wanting. Who but a God
Might live unscathed by sorrow all his days?
If I should tell those labours, the rough lodging,
The hard thwart's scant repose, the weary groans
That were our lot through watches of the day;
And then ashore ills more insufferable,
In camp beneath the beetling walls of Troy,
The rains from heaven and the dews that dripped
From sodden soils with cruel insistence, breeding
A host of vermin in our woollen cloaks;
If I should tell those winters, when the birds
Dropped dead and Ida heaped on us her snows,
Those summers, when unstirred by wind or wave
The sea lay pillowed in the sleep of noon—
But why lament that now? The toil is past—
Yes, for the dead so past that, where they lie,
No care shall trouble them to rise again.
Ah, those are spent: why count our losses then
And vex the quick with grievance of the dead?
So to adversity I bid farewell:
For us, survivors of the Argive arms,
Misfortune sinks, our vantage turns the scale.
And hence 'tis meet before yon rising sun
To cry o'er land and sea on wings of fame,
'Long since the Argive host which plundered Troy
Set up these spoils, a time-worn ornament,
Before this palace to the Gods of Greece.'
Whereto in answer should this land be praised
With those who led her, and to Zeus the giver
Shall thanks be given. That is all my news.

CHORUS: Well said! Your say, I grant you, masters mine.
Old age is ever young enough to learn.
This news, although it shall enrich me too,
Concerns the palace, and most of all the Queen.
(Clytemnestra appears at the door of the palace)

CLYTEMNESTRA: Long since I raised my joyful alleluias
When the first messenger flashed out of night
The tidings of the fall of Ilium,
And one rebuked me saying, 'Has a beacon
Persuaded you that Troy has now been taken?
Truly a woman's heart is light as air.'
Such was their gossip, and they called me mad;
But I still sacrificed, and through the town
The women's alleluia taken up
Was chanted gladly at the holy shrines,
Lulling to sleep the sacramental flame.
And now what need of further news from you?
I shall soon hear all from the King himself,
My honoured lord, for whom I shall prepare
A welcome home as fair as may be. What
Light could be sweeter in a woman's eyes
Than to fling wide the gates for her beloved
Whom God has saved from war? Go and command him
To hasten back, the darling of his people,
Where he shall find within his house a wife
As loyal as he left her, a faithful hound
Guarding his substance, to enemies unkind,
And in all else the same, his treasuries
Sealed all these years and still inviolate.
Delight from other men and ill-report
Are strange to me, as strange as tempered steel.
(She retires into the palace)

HERALD: Such is her boast, and though 'tis big with truth,
Is it not unseemly on a lady's lips?

CHORUS: Such is her message, as you understand,
To the instructed fair—in outward show.
But tell me, messenger, what of Menelaus,
Co-regent of this kingdom? Has he too
Returned in safety to his fatherland?

HERALD: I cannot tell a falsehood fair to bring
Enduring comfort to the friends I love.

CHORUS: Can you not make your tale both fair and true?
It is vain to hide disunion of the pair.

HERALD: The man has vanished from the Grecian host,
Himself and ship together. 'Tis the truth.

CHORUS: Did he embark from Troy before your eyes,
Or was it a storm that struck the fleet at sea?

HERALD: A skilful archer, you have hit the mark
And told a long disaster in a word.

CHORUS: But what report did rumour spread of him
Among the other seamen—alive or dead?

HERALD: We know not; none has certain news of him
Unless the Sun, from whom this earth draws life.

CHORUS: But tell us of that tempest that came down
So suddenly, a bolt from angry heaven.

HERALD: It is not meet to mar a day of praise
With voice of evil tidings: such offices
Are not for Gods of Heaven. When a man
Drags sadly home defeat long prayed-against,
With twofold wound, one of the commonwealth,
And one of each man driven from his home
Beneath that double scourge, the curse of War,
Armed with twin spears and double-braced for blood,
Such dire event were fit to celebrate
With some fell hymn to the infernal Furies;

But when he brings deliverance and finds
A land rejoicing in prosperity,—
How should I mingle foul with fair, and tell
Of tempest stirred out of an angry sky?
Water and Fire, old enemies before,
Conspired together and made covenant
To overwhelm the fated ships of Greece.
When night had fallen, with a rising swell,
The fleet was battered by the winds of Thrace,
Hull against hull, till, gorged and buffeted
With blasts of hail and blinding hurricane,
An evil shepherd swept them out of sight.
And when at last the sun's pale light arose,
We saw the Aegean in blossom with the strewn
Flotsam of drowning men and shattered spars.
Our own ship went unscathed; it must have been
Some deity that touched the helm and snatched
Or begged us off, and then the saving spirit
Of Fortune took the wheel, our pilot, till
We passed between the rugged mountain-cliffs
And anchored where we shipped the foam no more;
And there, delivered from that watery hell,
We nursed in brooding hearts the sudden stroke
That had laid our great armada in the dust.
And now, if any of those others live,
Why, they must deem that we are dead and gone.
As they of us, so we surmise of them.
But pray still for the best. And Menelaus,
Though likeliest far that he is in distress,
Still, if some ray of sunlight from above
Marks him among the living, rescued by Zeus
Reluctant that his seed should wholly perish,
Then there is hope yet for his safe return.
In this, believe me, you have heard the truth.

(The Herald returns to the army)

STR. 1

THIRD STASIMON

Who was he who named her name,
Justly called with perfect truth?
Surely one whom mortal eye may not see,
Prescient of her destiny,
Naming her with fatal chance
Bride of the lance and long dissension,
Helen—hell indeed she carried
Unto men and ships and a proud city, stealing
From the silk veils of her chamber, sailing seaward
With the Zephyr's breath behind her;
And the armed legions of men set out to hunt her
On the path that leaves no imprint
Till they beached on a leafy shore
Washed by Simois, bringing
War and the waste of bloodshed.

ANT. 1

Truly too for Ilium,
Turning into keeners kin,
Wrath, the instrument of God's will, at last
Claimed his payment for the spurned
Board of Zeus Hospitable,
Even from those who graced her nuptials
With the happy chant of Hymen
And acclaimed her coming with songs that soon were turned
into weeping.
They have learned another music
In the length of time, and cry out
In a loud voice for the sin of Paris, naming
Him the groom of black betrothal,
Mourning the guilt that laid them low in the dust of battle,
Stricken and steeped in bloodshed.

STR. 2

Of old, so it is said, an oxherd did rear at the hearth a young
Lion-cub, as a fosterling, in his infancy bringing

Smiles to the face of the aged,
Innocent sport of the children,
Often pampered and caressed,
Fondled like a babe with hands
Licked by the fawning tongue that craved
Meat from the master's table.

ANT. 2

But Time brought to the light his true nature, after his kind, and then
Years of care were repaid in slaughter of pasturing cattle,
Tearing the hand that had tended,
Blood in the house, and the inmates
Bowed in helpless anguish, struck
Down beneath the heaven-sent
Carnage which they had nursed, a fell
Priest of avenging bloodshed.

STR. 3

And so it seemed once there came to Ilium
A sweet-smiling calm, without cloud, serene, beguiling,
A rare gem set in crown of riches,
Shaft of a softly-glancing eye,
Bloom of love that doth prick the bosom.
But a change carried her bridals
To a bitter consummation.
To the proud children of Priam,
With the guidance | of the stern wrath
Of Zeus, she came as a fierce
Bridal-bewailing Fury.

(Clytemnestra appears at the door of the palace)

ANT. 3

A tale of old time is told on mortal lips,
That when man hath brought to full growth abundant riches,
It dies not childless, nay it breedeth;
Whence from a happy life is reaped

Fruit of plenteous lamentation.
With a lone voice I deny it.
It is only deeds unholy
That increase, fruitful in offspring
Of the same breed as its fathers.
Where justice rules in the house,
Blest of God is the issue.

STR. 4

But ancient pride loves to put forth a fresh bloom of sin out
of human evil, soon or late.
Behold, whenever the time appointed come,
A cloud of deep night, spirit of vengeance irresistible,
Horror of dark disaster hung
Brooding within the palace,
True to the dam that bore it.

ANT. 4

But where is Justice? She lights up the smoke-darkened hut,
yea she loves humility.
From gilded pinnacles of polluted hands
She turns her eyes back unto the dwelling of the pure in heart;
So, regarding not the false
Stamp on the face of wealth, leads
All to the end appointed.

(Enter Agamemnon riding in a chariot and followed by another which carries Cassandra and other spoils of war)

All hail, son of Atreus, captor of Troy,
All hail to thee, King!
How shall I greet thee, how tune my address
So as neither to fall too short nor surpass
Due measure of joy?
Full many are they who unjustly respect
Mere semblance of truth, and all men are quick
With a tear to the eye for a neighbour's distress,
But with hearts untouched by his trouble.

Just so they rejoice with him, forcing a smile
Like his on their laughterless faces.
Yet he that can read in the book of the eyes
Man's nature, will not be deluded by looks
Which fawn with dissembled fidelity, false
Like wine that is mingled with water.
So surely, I will not deny it, when thou
Didst marshal the host to recover
Helen, willingly wanton, with thousands of lives,
I accounted thee like to a picture deformed
Or a helm ill-turned by the pilot.
But now from the depth of the heart it is mine
To salute thee with love:
Toil happily crowned
Brings sweetness at last to the toiler.
And in time thou shalt learn to distinguish apart
The unjust and the just housekeeper among
Those who are set over thy people.

AGAMEMNON: First, it is just to greet this land of Argos
With her presiding Gods, my partners in
This homecoming, as in the just revenge
I brought to Priam's city. When the Gods
Heard that appeal unvoiced by mortal tongue,
They cast their votes decisive in the urn
Of blood with doom of death for Ilium
And uttermost destruction; and in the other
Hope hesitant still hovered on the brink.
The smoke of pillage marks that city yet,
The rites of ruin live. Her ashes breathe
Their last, with riches redolent, and die.
Wherefore 'tis right to render memorable
Thanks to the Gods. For that bold piracy
We have exacted payment; for a woman
That city lies in dust, struck by the fierce
Brood of the Horse, the Argive host in arms,

Which at the setting of the Pleiades
Leapt like a hungry lion across her towers
And slaked its thirst in streaming blood of kings.
Such is my measured preface to the Gods.
I have marked well your loyal sentiments
At one with mine, and sealed with my assent.
Too few are they whose nature is to honour
A friend's good fortune without jealousy.
Malignant venom seated at the heart
Doubles the sick man's burden, as he groans
For his own case and grieves no less to see
His neighbour walking in prosperity.
Devotion seeming-full—an empty shadow
I call it, speaking from sure knowledge tried
In the true mirror of companionship.
Odysseus only, who sailed against his will,
Once harnessed, proved a trusty outrigger—
Alive or dead, I know not. What concerns
The city and the Gods we shall dispose
In public congress, and deliberate
How what is well may be continued so,
And where some sickness calls for remedy,
We shall with cautery or kindly knife
Of surgery essay to heal the sore.
But now, returning to my royal hearth,
My first act shall be to salute the Gods
Who led me hence and lead me home again;
Victory attends me: may she rest secure!

CLYTEMNESTRA: People of Argos, elders assembled here,
I shall declare before you unashamed
My way with him I love; for diffidence
Dies in us all with time. I tell a tale
From my own heart of the unhappy life
I led while he fought under Ilium.
First, none can say how much a wife must bear,

Who sits at home, with no man's company,
And waits upon the train of evil news,
One messenger, then another with a tale
Of worse disaster shouted through the house;
And as for wounds, if he had met as many
As constant rumour poured into his home,
His limbs were like a net, pierced through and through.
If he had died, the prevalent report,
He was a second Geryon, with bodies three
And triple cloak of earth draped over them,
Three outstretched corpses and one death for each.
Beset with malignant rumours such as these,
Often the halter pressed my eager throat,
Released by others with no thanks from me.
And hence it is our child is not here present,
As it were meet, pledge of our plighted vows,
Orestes. Marvel not at this. He lives
Safe in the charge of an old friend at arms,
Strophius the Phocian, who admonished me
Of various dangers—your life in jeopardy,
A restive populace, and that fault of nature,
When man has been cast down, to trample on him.
In this excuse, believe me, lies the truth.
As for myself, the fountains of my tears
Are drained away till not a drop is left.
The late night-vigils have outworn my eyes,
Weeping the light that was to burn for you,
With tears that went unheeded. Even in dreams
I would start up, roused by the tenuous beat
Of a gnat's wing from visions all of you,
Imagining more ills than credible
In the slow hours that kept me company.
But now, all griefs endured with patient heart,
I name this man the watchdog of the fold,
Forestay that saves the ship, upsoaring oak
That holds the roof, a longed-for only child,

A shore unhoped-for spied by sailors' eyes!
This is my greeting, this my homage to him,
And may no envy follow it! Enough
Our sorrows heretofore; and now, beloved,
Step from the chariot, but do not set
Upon the ground those feet that trampled Troy.
Make haste, my handmaids who have been appointed
To strew his path with outspread tapestry.
Prepare a road of purple coverlets
Where Justice leads to an unhoped-for home;
And there the rest our sleep-unvanquished care
Shall order justly, as the Gods ordain.

AGAMEMNON: Daughter of Leda, guardian of my home,
Your greeting was prolonged, proportionate
To my long absence; but tributes of due praise
Should come from other lips; and furthermore
Seek not to unman me with effeminate
Graces and barbarous salaams agape
In grovelling obeisance at my feet,
Nor with invidious purple pave my way.
Such honours are an appanage of God,
And I, being mortal, cannot but fear to tread
On this embroidered beauty, rich and rare.
Honour me as a man, not as a God.
Foot-mats and fine robes ring differently
In Rumour's ill-tongued music, and of all
God's gifts the chief is wisdom. Count him blest
Whose life has ended in felicity.
I shall act as I have told you, conscience-clear.

CLYTEMNESTRA: Yet tell me frankly, according to your
judgment—

AGAMEMNON: My judgment stands, make no mistake of that.

CLYTEMNESTRA: Would you in danger have vowed to God
this act?

AGAMEMNON: Yes, if the priesthood had commanded it.

CLYTEMNESTRA: And what, if Priam had conquered, would *he* have done?

AGAMEMNON: He would have trod the purple, I do not doubt.

CLYTEMNESTRA: Then give no thought to mortal tongues that wag.

AGAMEMNON: The clamour of a populace counts for much.

CLYTEMNESTRA: Whom no man envies, no man shall admire.

AGAMEMNON: It is not for a woman to take part in strife.

CLYTEMNESTRA: Well may the victor yield a victory!

AGAMEMNON: Do *you* set store by such a victory?

CLYTEMNESTRA: Be tempted, freely vanquished, victor still!

AGAMEMNON: Well, if it be your will, let someone loose
The sandals bound in service to my feet;
And as they tread this ocean-purple, may
No far-off God cast on me envious eyes!
Deep shame there lies in prodigality
Which tramples robes woven of silver worth.
But be it so. And see this stranger here
Is treated gently. Kingship kindly used
Wins favour in the sight of God above;
For no man willingly endures the yoke
Of servitude, and she, the army's gift,
Is a blossom culled out of uncounted wealth.
And now, constrained to accept these honours from you,
Treading the purple I pass into my home.

CLYTEMNESTRA: There is still the sea, it shall not be dried up,
Renewing fresh from infinite abundance
Rich merchandise of purple-stained attire;
Wherein the Gods, my lord, have well endowed
A royal house that knows no penury.

How many robes would I have vowed to tread,
Had prophecy instructed, if thereby
I had contrived the ransom of one soul!
While the root lives, the foliage shall raise
Its shady arch against the burning Dog-star;
And, as your coming to your hearth and home
Signifies warmth that comes in wintry cold,
So, when Zeus from the bitter virgin-grape
Draws wine, then coolness fills the house at last,
As man made perfect moves about his home.

(Agamemnon has gone into the palace)

Zeus, Zeus the Perfecter, perfect thou my prayer,
And perfect also that which is thy care!

(Clytemnestra goes into the palace)

STR. I

FOURTH STASIMON

What is this insistent fear
Which in my prophetic heart
Set and steady beats with evil omen,
Chanting unbidden a brooding, oracular music?
Why can I not cast it out
Like a dream of dark import,
Setting good courage firm
On my spirit's empty throne?
In time the day came
When the Greeks, with anchors plunged
Deep in that shingle strand,
Moored the sloops of war, and men
Thronged the beach of Ilium;

ANT. I

So to-day my eyes have seen
Safe at last their homecoming.
Still I hear a strain of stringless music,
Dissonant dirge of the Furies, a chant uninstructed
Quired in this uneasy breast,

Desolate of hope and cheer.
Not for naught beats the heart
Stirred with ebb and flow of fate
In righteous men: soon
What is feared shall come to pass.
Yet against hope I pray,
May it prove of no import,
Unfulfilled and falsified!

STR. 2

If a man's health be advanced over the due mean,
It will trespass soon upon sickness who stands
Close neighbour, between them a thin wall.
So doth the passage of life
Sped with a favouring breeze
Suddenly founder on reefs of destruction.
Caution seated at the helm
Casts a portion of the load
Overboard with measured throw.
So the ship shall come to shore;
So the house shall stand, if not
Overcharged with store of woe.
Plenty from Zeus and abundance that yieldeth a yearly return
    from the harvested furrows
Driveth hunger from the door.

ANT. 2

But if the red blood of a man ever be spilled on the ground,
    dripping and deadly, then who
Shall recall it again with his magic?
Even the healer who knew
Charms to recover the dead,
Zeus put an end to his wrongful powers.
Portions are there preordained,
Each supreme within its own
Bounds decreed eternally;
Else would heart outstripping tongue

Cast misgiving to the winds.
Now in darkness deep it groans,
Brooding in sickly despair, and no longer it hopes to resolve
in an orderly web these
Mazes of a fevered mind.

(Clytemnestra appears at the door of the palace)

CLYTEMNESTRA: You too, Cassandra, come within; for Zeus
Of his great mercy grants to you a part
In our domestic sacrifice, to stand
Among the slaves before his altar there.
Step from the chariot, put by your pride.
Even great Heracles submitted once
To toil and eat the bread of slavery;
And should compulsion bring a man to this,
Much comfort lies in service to a house
Of immemorial riches. Those who have reaped
A harvest never hoped-for out of hand
Are strict upon the rule and show no mercy.
What is customary shall here be yours.

CHORUS: To you she spoke, and made her meaning plain.
Caught in the casting-net of destiny,
'Twere best to yield; and yet perchance you will not.

CLYTEMNESTRA: Nay, if she speak not, like the
babbling swallow,
Some barbarous tongue which none can understand,
With mystic words I'll win the mind within.

CHORUS: Go with her. Your plight affords no better choice.
Step from the chariot and do her will.

CLYTEMNESTRA: I have no time to idle at the door.
The victims stand upon the palace hearth
Before the altar, ready for the knife
To render thanks for these unhoped-for joys.
If you too will take part, do not delay;

But, if you lack the wit to understand me,
Do *you* address her with barbarian hand.

CHORUS: She needs, it seems, a clear interpreter.
Like some wild creature is she, newly-trapped.

CLYTEMNESTRA: Nay, she is mad, and gives her ears to folly.
Her city newly-captured, hither brought
A slave, she knows not how to take the bit
Until her pride is foamed away in blood.
I'll waste no more words to demean myself.
(Clytemnestra goes into the palace)

CHORUS: *I* feel no anger, for I pity you.
Unhappy girl, dismount and follow her,
Yield to your fate and take its yoke upon you.

STR. I KOMMOS
CASSANDRA: Oh! Alas, Earth! Apollo, Apollo!

CHORUS: What is this cry in the name of Loxias?
He is not one to greet with lamentation.

ANT. I
CASSANDRA: Oh! Alas, Earth! Apollo, Apollo!

CHORUS: Again she calls with blasphemous utterance
The God who stands aloof from mourning cries.

STR. 2
CASSANDRA: Apollo, Apollo, the Wayfarer! Destroyed by thee!
Once more hast thou destroyed me wantonly!

CHORUS: Her own sad fate, it seems, she will prophesy.
She is now a slave, and yet God's gift abides.

ANT. 2
CASSANDRA: Apollo, Apollo, the Wayfarer! Destroyed by thee!
Ah, whither hast thou led me? What house is this?

CHORUS: The House of the Atreidae. Nay, if that
Thou knowest not, then hear the truth from me.

STR. 3

CASSANDRA: Palace abhorred of God, conscious of hidden crime,
Sanguinary, sullied with slaughtered kin,
A charnel-house that streams with children's blood!

CHORUS: Keen as a hound upon the scent she seems,
This stranger, tracking down a murderous trail.

ANT. 3

CASSANDRA: I can declare a testimony plain to read.
Listen to them as they lament the foul
Repast of roasted flesh for father's mouth!

CHORUS: We know of thy prophetic fame already,
And have no need of an interpreter.

STR. 4

CASSANDRA: Out, out, alas! What is it plotted now?
Horror unspeakable
Is plotted in this house, insufferable,
A hard cross for kinsfolk,
Without cure. The hoped-for succour is far away.

CHORUS: This prophecy escapes me. Yet the first
I recognised—the country cries of it.

ANT. 4

CASSANDRA: Alas, O wicked! Is thy purpose *that*?
He who hath shared thy bed,
To bathe his limbs, to smile—how speak the end?
The end comes, and quickly:
A hand reaching out, followed by a hand again!

CHORUS: Still at a loss am I; riddles before,
Now sightless oracles obscure my way.

STR. 5

CASSANDRA: Ah, ah! O horrible!
What is appearing now? Some net of mesh infernal.
Mate of his bed and board, she is a snare
Of slaughter! Oh, murderous ministers,
Cry alleluia, cry,
Fat with blood, dance and sing!

STR. 6

CHORUS: What is this Fury thou hast called to cry
In exultation? It brings no cheer to me.
Oh, to the heart it falls, saffron of hue, the drop
Of blood which doth sink with life's setting sun,
Smitten with edge of steel.
Nearer, yet nearer draws the swift judgment-stroke.

ANT. 5

CASSANDRA: Ah, ah! Beware, beware!
Let not the cow come near! See how the bull is captured!
She wraps him in the robe, the hornèd trap,
Then strikes. He falls into the bath, the foul
Treacherous bowl of blood. Such her skilled artistry.

ANT. 6

CHORUS: No gift I boast in reading prophecy,
But this must signify calamity.
When did a prophet's voice issue in happiness?
Amidst mortal stress his word-woven art,
Ever divining ill,
Teacheth mankind before the hour chants of fear.

STR. 7

CASSANDRA: Alas, alas, unhappy, pitiful destiny!
Now I lament my own passion to fill the bowl.
Oh whither hast thou led me? O my grief,
Whither, unless that I with him must die?

STR. 8

CHORUS: Spirit of frenzy borne on by the breath of God,
Thy own mournful dirge
Singest thou, like the red-brown bird
Who never-weary pours out her full heart in song;
Itys, Itys! she cries, sorrow hath filled her days,
The sad nightingale.

ANT. 7

CASSANDRA: Alas, alas, the sweet music of the nightingale!
Body of wings the Gods fashioned to cover her,
And gave her, free of weeping, happy days.
For me there waits the stroke of two-edged steel.

ANT. 8

CHORUS: Whence is this passionate madness inspired of God
That still streameth on?
Tales of fear told in uncouth cries,
Set to a strain of high-pitched and harsh harmonies?
Whither the path of wild prophecy evil-tongued?
O where must it end?

STR. 9

CASSANDRA: O fatal bridal-day, Paris the curse of all his kin!
O swift Scamander, streaming past my home,
Once on the banks of those waters I dwelt, and they
Nourished me as a child.
But now, it seems, my cries shall soon resound
Beside Cocytus and sad Acheron.

STR. 10

CHORUS: What is it now? A cry simple for all to read.
Even a child may understand.
With sharp anguish cleft, as though red with blood,
My heart breaks, as these pitiful plaintive cries
Shatter the listening soul.

ANT. 9

CASSANDRA: Alas the pain, the pain, agony of a plundered town!
Alas, the King's rich offerings at the gates,
Lavished from flocks and herds, little availed to bring
Help to the city, so
That she might not have been what she is now.
And I distraught shall dash into the snare.

ANT. 10

CHORUS: Like to the rest is this pitiful utterance.
What evil spirit hath possessed
Thy soul, cruelly bending those fevered lips
To give voice to such dolorous tunes of death?
Who shall divine the end?

CASSANDRA: Listen! No more my prophecy shall glance
As through a veil, like a new-wedded maid.
Nay, bright and fresh, I tell thee, it shall flow
Against the sunrise, and like a wave engulf
The daybreak in disaster greater far
Than this. No riddles now; I shall instruct,
And you shall bear me witness step by step,
As I track down the scent of crimes of old.
On yonder housetop ever abides a choir
Of minstrels unmelodious, singing of ill;
And deeply-drunk, to fortify their spirit,
In human blood, those revellers yet abide,
Whom none can banish, Furies congenital,
And settled on the roof they chant the tune
Of old primordial Ruin, each in turn
Spewing with horror at a brother's outraged bed.
Say, have I missed, or marked my quarry down?
Am I a false prophet babbling at the gates?
Bear me on oath your witness that I know
The story of this household's ancient crimes.

CHORUS: What could an oath, however truly sworn,

Avail to heal? Indeed I marvel at you,
Born far beyond the sea, speaking of this,
An alien country, as though you had been present.

CASSANDRA: The seer Apollo bestowed that gift upon me.

CHORUS: Was he smitten with the shaft of love, a God?

CASSANDRA: Time was, shame would not let me speak of this.

CHORUS: Prosperity makes man fastidious.

CASSANDRA: Oh, but he wrestled strenuously for my love.

CHORUS: Did he bring you to the act of getting child?

CASSANDRA: First I consented, then I cheated him.

CHORUS: Already captive to his craft divine?

CASSANDRA: Already I foretold my people's fate.

CHORUS: How did you find refuge from his displeasure?

CASSANDRA: The price I paid was that none gave me heed.

CHORUS: Your prophecies have earned belief from us.

CASSANDRA: Oh misery!
Again the travail of true prophecy
With prelude wild makes tumult in my soul!
Do you not see them, seated on the roof,
Those children, like the ghastly shapes of dreams,
Murdered, it seems, by their own kith and kin,
Meat in their hands from some familiar meal,
The inward parts and bowels, of which their father
Ate—what a pitiable load is theirs!
That is the sin for which is planned revenge
By the faint-hearted lion, stretched in the bed,
Who keeps house for my master—being his slave,
I must needs name him so—now home again.
Little he knows what that foul bitch, with ears

Laid back and lolling tongue, will bring to pass
With vicious snap of treacherous destruction.
So dead to shame! woman to murder man!
What beast abominable is her name?
Double-faced amphisbene, or skulking Scylla
Among the cliffs, waylaying mariners,
A hellish dam raging against her own,
In strife that gives no quarter! How loud she sang
Her alleluias over the routed foe,
While feigning gladness at his safe return!
Believe me not, what matter? 'Tis all one.
The future comes, and when your eyes have seen,
You shall cry out in pity, 'She spoke true.'

CHORUS: Thyestes' banquet of the flesh of babes
I understood, and shuddered, terrified
To hear that tale told with unerring truth;
But for the rest I wander far astray.

CASSANDRA: I say you shall see Agamemnon's death.

CHORUS: Unhappy girl, hush those ill-omened lips!

CASSANDRA: No healing god is here—there is no cure.

CHORUS: None, if it be so; and yet may it not be!

CASSANDRA: While you are praying, others prepare to kill.

CHORUS: What man would plot so foul a villainy?

CASSANDRA: Ah, you have missed my meaning utterly.

CHORUS: But who shall do it? That escapes me still.

CASSANDRA: And yet I know too well the speech of Greece.

CHORUS: So does the Delphian, yet are his sayings dark.

CASSANDRA: Ah, how it burns, the fire! It sweeps upon me!
Oh, oh! Apollo! Oh alas, my sorrow!
That lioness two-footed, lying with
The wolf in absence of the noble lion,

Shall kill me, O unhappy, and as though
Mixing a potion pours in the cup of wrath
My wages too, and while she sets an edge
Upon the steel for him, she vows to make
Murder the price of my conveyance hither.
Why do I wear these tawdry mockeries,
This staff, this mantic wreath about my neck?
If I must die, then you shall perish first.
Down to perdition! Now you have your pay.
Bestow your fatal riches on another!
Behold Apollo stripping me himself
Of my prophetic raiment, regarding me,
Clad in his robes, a public laughing-stock
Of friend and enemy, one who has endured
The name of witch, waif, beggar, castaway.
So now the seer who made these eyes to see
Has led his servant to this mortal end.
No altar of my fathers waits for me,
But a block that drips blood at a dead man's grave.
And yet we die not unavenged of heaven.
Another shall come to avenge us both,
Who for his father's sake shall kill his mother,
A wandering outcast, an exile far away,
He shall come back and set for his kin a crown
On this long tale of ruin. The Gods above
Have sworn a solemn covenant that his
Dead father's outstretched corpse shall call him home.
Why do I weep for this so piteously?
Have I not seen the fall of Ilium?
And those who laid that city waste are thus
Discharged at last by heaven's arbitrament.
This door I name the gate of Hades: now
I will go and knock, I will endure to die.
My only prayer is that the blow be mortal,
To close these eyes in sleep without a struggle,
While my life's blood ebbs peacefully away.

CHORUS: O woman in whose wisdom is much grief,
Long have you spoken; and yet, if you know
The end, why like the consecrated ox
Walk with such patient step into the slaughter?

CASSANDRA: Should the end linger, that is no escape.

CHORUS: And yet the latest moment is the best.

CASSANDRA: What should I gain by flight? My hour has come.

CHORUS: You have the endurance of a valiant heart.

CASSANDRA: Such words are common for those whom life has crossed.

CHORUS: Yet there is comfort in honourable death.

CASSANDRA: O father, father, and thy noble sons!
(Cassandra approaches the door, then recoils)

CHORUS: What is it? What terror has turned you back?

CASSANDRA: Faugh!

CHORUS: What means that cry? Some sickening at the heart?

CASSANDRA: The palace reeks with fumes of dripping blood.

CHORUS: No, 'tis the smell of fireside sacrifice.

CASSANDRA: A vapour such as issues from a tomb.

CHORUS: No scent of Araby have you marked in it.

CASSANDRA: Nay, I will go to weep inside the house
Agamemnon's fate and mine. Enough of life!
O hear me, friends!
I am not scared like a bird once limed that takes
Fright at a bush. Witness, when I am dead,
The day when woman for this woman dies
And man mismarried for a man lies low.
I beg this of you at the point of death.

CHORUS: Poor soul, foredoomed to death, I pity you.

CASSANDRA: Yet one word more I have to speak, my own
Dirge for myself. I pray the Sun in heaven,
On whom I look my last, that he may grant
To him who shall come to avenge my master
From those who hate me payment of the price
For this dead slave-girl slain with so light a stroke.
Alas, mortality! when fortunate,
A painted image; in adversity,
The sponge's moist touch wipes it all away.

CHORUS: And this to me is far more pitiable.
(Cassandra goes into the palace)

Good fortune among mankind is a thing
Insatiable. Mansions of kings are marked
By the fingers of all, none warns her away,
None cries, O enter not hither!
Unto him the Immortals accorded the fall
Of the city of Troy,
And with honours divine he returns to his home.
But now, if the debt of the blood of the past
Is on him, if his death must crown it and pay
To the dead their price for the slaughtered of old,
Then who, when he hears these things, is assured
Of a life unwounded of sorrow?

AGAMEMNON: Oh me, I am struck down!

CHORUS: Hark, did you not hear that cry? The stroke of death!

AGAMEMNON: Oh me, again!

CHORUS: Ah, his voice it is, our King! The deed is done.
Come, take counsel how to meet this perilous hour.
1. I say, raise hue and cry—rally the people!
2. Break in at once upon their dripping blade.
3. Yes, let us act—no time for faltering now.

4. This bloody deed spells tyranny to come.
5. *They* spurn delay—*their* hands are not asleep.
6. What can we do, old men whose strength is gone?
7. No words of ours can raise the dead to life.
8. Must we wear out our age in slavery?
9. No, death is gentler than the tyrant's lash.
10. We heard his cries, but his death is still unproved.
11. Yes, we are only guessing—we must know.
12. Agreed, to find how is it with the King.

(As the old men are about to enter the palace, the doors are thrown open: Clytemnestra is seen standing over the bodies of Agamemnon and Cassandra, which are laid out on a purple robe)

CLYTEMNESTRA: Now I shall feel no shame to contradict
All that was said before to bide my time.
How else should one who pondered on revenge
Against a covert enemy, have strung the snare
Of death so high as to outsoar his leaping?
This duel, nurtured in my thoughts so long,
Is crowned at last with perfect victory.
I stand here, where I struck, over my work.
And it was so contrived, I'll not deny,
To leave no fissure, no escape from death.
With this vast net, as might be cast for fish,
I sieged him round in the fatal wealth of purple,
And twice I struck him, and with two cries of pain
He stretched his legs; then on his fallen body
I gave the third blow, my drink-offering
To the Zeus of Hell, Deliverer of the dead.
There he lay prostrate, gasping out his soul,
And pouring forth a sudden spurt of blood
Rained thick these drops of deathly dew upon me,
While I rejoiced like cornfields at the flow
Of heavenly moisture in birth-pangs of the bud.
So stands the case, elders of Argos, so
Rejoice, if so it please you—I glory in it.

For if due offerings were his to drink,
Then those were justly his, and more than just.
With bitter tears he filled the household bowl,
Now he himself has drained it and is gone.

CHORUS: I marvel at your tongue so brazen-bold
That dares to speak so of your murdered king.

CLYTEMNESTRA: You trifle with me as with a foolish woman,
While, nothing daunted, to such as understand
I say—commend or censure, as you will,
It is no matter—here is Agamemnon,
My husband, dead, the work of this right hand,
A just artificer. That is the truth.

STR. I

CHORUS: Woman, what evil charm bred out of earth or
flowing sea,
Poison to eat or drink, hast thou devoured to take
On thee a crime that cries out for a public curse?
'Twas thine, the stroke, the blow—banishment shall be thine,
Hissed and hated of all men.

CLYTEMNESTRA: Your sentence now is banishment for me,
Abhorred of all, cursed and abominated;
But you did nothing then to contravene
His purpose, when, to exorcise the storms,
As though it were a ewe picked from his flocks
Whose wealth of snowy fleeces never fails
To multiply, unmoved, he killed his own
Child, born to me in pain, my well-beloved.
Why did you not drive *him* from hearth and home
For that foul crime, reserving your stern judgment
Until *I* acted? I bid you cast at me
Such menaces as will make for mastery
In combat match for match with one who stands
Prepared to meet them; and if with the help of God

The issue goes against you, suffering
Shall school those gray hairs in humility.

ANT. I

CHORUS: Spirit of wickedness and haughty utterance! As now
Over the drops of red murder the mind doth rave,
So doth a fleck of red blood in the eyes appear.
Dishonoured and deserted of thy friends, for this
Stroke soon shalt thou be stricken.

CLYTEMNESTRA: Hark to the sanction of my solemn oath.
By perfect Justice who avenged my child,
By Ruin and the Fury unto whom
I slew this sacramental offering,
No thought of fear shall walk beneath this roof,
While on my hearth the fire is kindled by
Aegisthus, faithful to me from of old,
A shield and buckler strong in my defence.
Low lies the man that shamed his wedded wife,
Sweet solace of the Trojan Chryseids,
And stretched beside him this prisoner of war,
His paramour, this visionary seer,
His faithful bedfellow, who fondled him
On the ship's benches. Both have their deserts—
He as you see him; she like a swan has sung
Her last sad roundelay, and, lying there,
His leman, a side-dish for his nuptial bed,
She brings to me the spice that crowns my joy.

STR. 2

CHORUS: Oh for the gift of death, speedy and free of pain,
Free from watch at the sick-bed,
To bring the long sleep that knows no waking,
Now that my lord and loyal protector
Lieth slain. For woman's sake
Long he warred far away while he lived,
Now at home dies beneath a woman's hand.

O Helen, oh folly-beguiled,
One woman to take those thousands of lives
That were lost in the land of the Trojans,
Now thou hast set on the curse of the household
A crown of blood beyond ablution.
Such the world has never known,
Spirit of strife strong in man's destruction!

CLYTEMNESTRA: Pray not for the portion of death, though sore
Distressed is thy heart,
Nor turn upon Helen the edge of thy wrath,
Saying that she slew men without number,
One woman, a wound that shall close not.

ANT. 2

CHORUS: Demon of blood and tears, swooping upon the two
Tribes of Tantalus' children,
Enthroned in two women single-hearted,
Victor art thou, and my soul is stricken.
See on the palace-roof he stands,
Like the foul raven, evil-tongued,
Hear him croak, jubilant, his chant of joy!

CLYTEMNESTRA: Ah, now is a true thought framed on thy lips,
Naming this demon
Thrice fed on the race, who, glutted with blood,
With the old wound smarting, is craving to lap
Fresh blood, still young in his hunger.

STR. 3

CHORUS: Demon of sudden destruction,
Laying the house in the dust for ever!
Oh me, 'tis an evil tale of ruin that never resteth.
Alas, I weep the will of Zeus
Who causeth all and worketh all;
For what without his will befalleth mortals,
And what here was not sent from heaven?
Oh me, I weep for my master and king.

How shall I mourn thee?
What words shall a fond heart speak thee?
In the coils of the spider, the web of a death
Ungodly, entangled thou diest.
Oh me, I lament thy unkingly bed,
With a sudden stroke of sharp
Two-edged treachery felled and slaughtered.

CLYTEMNESTRA: Why dost thou declare that the murder was mine?
Name it not so, nor
Call me Agamemnon's wife. 'Tis not I
But a ghost in the likeness of woman, the vengeful
Shade of the banqueter whom Atreus fed,
Now crowneth his own
Firstfruits with a perfect oblation.

ANT. 3

CHORUS: How art thou guiltless of murder?
None is there, none that shall bear thee witness.
No, no, but perchance some ancient shade of wrath was abettor.
'Tis onward driven, stream on stream
Of slaughter sprung from common seed,
Murder red, that soon shall move to ransom
The dried gore of the flesh of children.
Oh me, I weep for my master and king.
How shall I mourn thee?
What words shall a fond heart speak thee?
In the coils of the spider, the web of a death
Ungodly, entangled thou diest.
Oh me, I lament thy unkingly bed,
With a sudden stroke of sharp
Two-edged treachery felled and slaughtered.

CLYTEMNESTRA: What of *him*? Did he not set ruin afoot
In the house when he slew

Iphigeneia, the child that I bore him?
And with long bitter tears have I mourned her.
So has he done, so is he done by.
Let him not speak proudly in darkness below.
With the death of the sword
For the sin of the sword he has perished.

STR. 4

CHORUS: Alas, the mind strays disarmed, resourceless;
Weakly it drifts, and whither
To turn it knows not. The house is falling.
I fear the sharp beat of blood will soon have laid
The roof in ruins. The storm is growing.
Another mortal stroke for Justice' hand
Is now made sharp on other whetstones.
Alas, Earth, Earth, would thou hadst taken
This body before I had looked on my lord
Laid low in the vessel of silver.
Oh me, who shall bury him, who shall lament?
Or wilt thou have the heart, having murdered thy own
Master, to mourn at his tomb and to offer
To his spirit a gift unacceptable, such
Unholy return for his great deeds?
Who shall intone at the tomb of a blessed spirit
Tearful psalms of salutation,
A tribute pure in heart and truthful?

CLYTEMNESTRA: That office is nothing to you—it is mine.
I struck him and killed him, I'll bury him too,
But not with mourners from home in his train,
No, Iphigeneia, his daughter shall come,
As is meet, to receive him, her father, beside
Those waters of wailing, and throwing her arms
On his neck with a kiss she shall greet him.

ANT. 4

CHORUS: The charge is answered with counter-charges.

Who shall be judge between them?
The spoiler spoiled, slaughtered he who slaughtered.
The law abides yet beside the throne of Zeus,
The sinner must suffer. So 'tis ordered.
The seed accurst, O who shall drive it out?
The whole house falleth, nailed to ruin.

CLYTEMNESTRA: So naming the law, truth hast thou spoken.
As for me, I consent
On my oath to the demon that haunteth the house
To endure ills present, though heavy to bear;
Let him now go hence
And inflict upon others the burden of blood
Outpoured by the hand of a kinsman.
Then would a scanty
Pittance content me better than plenty,
As the house is absolved
From the madness of murder for murder.
(Enter Aegisthus with a bodyguard)

AEGISTHUS: O kindly light, O day of just reward,
Now have I proof there are avenging Gods
Who look down from above on human sin,
As I regard these purple snares of hell
Wherein to my delight this man doth lie,
Distrained by death for a father's treachery.
His father, Atreus, monarch of this realm,
Challenged in right of sovranty by mine,
Thyestes, his own brother, banished him
From hearth and home. A suppliant, he returned,
And found such safety for himself as not
To stain his native soil with his own blood;
But wicked Atreus, courteous more than kind,
Regaled him at a festive holiday
To a banquet of his children's flesh. The toes
And fingers set aside, the rest was laid
Disguised before him, where he sat apart.

My father unsuspecting took and ate—
A banquet prodigal in calamity
For this whole house. As soon as he divined
The monstrous crime, with a loud cry he fell
Back, spewing out the slaughtered flesh,
And cursed the House of Pelops—with a kick
That threw the table to the floor he cried,
'So perish all the seed of Pleisthenes!'
That is the sin for which this man lies here.
And that the plot should have been spun by me
Is also just; for, when I was a child
In swaddling-clothes, my father's third last hope,
I was condemned with him to banishment,
Till Justice reared me up and brought me home.
And so, though absent, still the blow was mine,
Mine were the threads of the conspiracy.
And now to die were sweet, since I have seen
My enemy caught by Justice in her snares.

CHORUS: Aegisthus, insult in an evil hour
Wins no respect from me. If it be true
You killed with full intent, if you alone
Contrived this deed of bloodshed from afar,
Then be assured, your head shall not escape
The stones of an indignant people's curse.

AEGISTHUS: Such talk from lower benches to the helm
Of high command! 'Tis hard, as you shall find,
For age to learn, and yet you shall be taught.
Even in dotage, dungeons and the pangs
Of hunger make an excellent physician
To school the spirit. Have you not eyes to see?
Kick not against the pricks, or smart for it!

CHORUS: Woman! A man returned from feats of war,
While you kept house at home and fouled his bed,
A great commander—*you* contrived his death!

AEGISTHUS: More talk that shall yet prove the seed of tears!
The tongue of Orpheus, contrary to yours,
Led all in listening rapture after him;
But you, a nuisance with your senseless bark,
Chains shall instruct you in docility.

CHORUS: What? *you* my master, *you* tyrant of the land,
Who, though the plot was yours, yet lacked the courage
To raise a hand to execute the plot!

AEGISTHUS: Plainly, temptation was the woman's part;
I, as his ancient enemy, was suspect.
But now, with his possessions, I shall try
My hand at monarchy. Who disobeys
Shall groan beneath the yoke—no trace-horse he
Pampered with corn; no, slow starvation walled
In noisome darkness shall see him humbled yet.

CHORUS: O craven spirit, who had no heart to kill
But left it to a woman, who defiles
Her Gods and country! Oh, does Orestes yet
Behold the light of life, that he may come
Favoured of fortune home, and prove himself
The sovran executioner of both?

AEGISTHUS: So? If you are bent on folly, you shall soon be taught.
Ho, my trusty guards, come forward, here is work to do.

CAPTAIN OF THE GUARD: Ho, let each man draw and hold his sword in readiness!

CHORUS: Be it so, we too are ready, unafraid to die.

AEGISTHUS: Die! Well-spoken, we shall gladly take you at your word.

CLYTEMNESTRA: Peace! my lord, forbear, and let no further ill be done.
Rich already is the harvest of calamity.

Grief is ours in plenty—draw no blood to make it more.
Go your ways, old men, and bow to destiny in due
Season, lest you suffer. What has been, it had to be.
Should this penance prove sufficient, though we bear the scars
Of an evil spirit's talons, we shall rest content.
Such the counsel of a woman; pray, be ruled by me.

AEGISTHUS: Must I listen to their wanton threats of violence,
Flowers of insolence wherewith they trifle with their fate,
So bereft of sense they know not who is master here?

CHORUS: Men of Argos are not used to cringe before a knave.

AEGISTHUS: I shall overtake you yet—the reckoning is nigh.

CHORUS: Not if saving fortune guide Orestes home again.

AEGISTHUS: Yes, I know the only food of castaways is hope.

CHORUS: Gloat and grow fat, brag and blacken Justice while
you dare!

AEGISTHUS: Soon the hour shall come when foolish talk shall
cost you dear.

CHORUS: Flaunt your feathers, fluster like a cock beside his hen!

CLYTEMNESTRA: Do not heed their idle clamour. You and I,
the new
Masters of the house, henceforward shall direct it well.

CHOEPHOROE

CHARACTERS

ORESTES
PYLADES
ELECTRA
CLYTEMNESTRA
AEGISTHUS
A SERVANT
A NURSE
CHORUS

CHOEPHOROE

(The scene as before. Enter Orestes and Pylades)

ORESTES: Hermes, whose home is in the earth, whose eyes
Look down on my paternal heritage,
Deliver me, do battle by my side!
Unto my country I return, restored.

And now beside my father's tomb I call
On him to hear and hearken.

A lock to Inachus who nurtured me,
And now another in token of my grief.

I was not present, father, to lament
Thy death nor raise a hand in sorrow, when
They brought thy body from the house.

(A cry is heard within. Electra and the Chorus of serving-women come out of the palace)

What do I see? What gathering is this
Of women clad in robes of sombre hue?
What sad occasion calls them? Can it be
A new affliction laid upon the house,
Or for my father, shall I say, they bring
Drink-offerings to propitiate the dead?
So it must be; for now I think I see
Electra too, my sister, walking bowed
In heavy grief. O Zeus, may I avenge
My father's death! Defend and fight for me!
Pylades, let us stand aside, until
We know the meaning of this act of prayer.

STR. I

PARODOS

I issue from the house to bring
Oblations forth with blow of beating hand.
Behold, my streaming cheek is freshly furrowed
Red and rent with cruel nail.
On grief's shrill cries my sick heart doth feed continually.
The sundered linen shrieketh loud in tune with lamentation; so
Raiment torn lays bare
Twin breasts to the beating palm for this occasion sad.

ANT. I

A cry was heard, it pierced the night,
Prophetic terror breathing wrath to come;
Hair-raising panic swiftly scattered slumber,
Heavy, haunting shriek of fear;
It rang out loud and shrill, where the women's chambers are.
And then the prophets taught of God, after they had read
the dream,
Cried out their message:
Dead men in the earth are wroth with those who
murdered them.

STR. 2

Now to placate such ills implacable—
O hear, Earth, Mother!—fearful she hath sent me,
Godless woman! Nay, I dread e'en to utter such a name.
When blood is spilt, atonement is there none.
Alas, O sorrow-smitten home!
Alas, O roof in ruin laid,
Engulfed in these accursèd shades
Of sunless night, which have been drawn
Down by death of thy master!

ANT. 2

Respect for power unmatched in battle once,
In all ears and hearts public and pervasive,
Now hath drawn aside, and men fear; for happy fortune is

A God in mortal eyes and more than God.
And yet the scale of Justice stands
And watches, swift to visit some
In life, for others pain abides
In twilit realms, while on the rest
Night descends everlasting.

STR. 3

When blood is shed and drunk by mother Earth,
The vengeful gore congeals immovable.
Slow-paced judgment beareth the offender on, till grief
Glut his greedy appetite.

ANT. 3

As he who treads the virgin bower can find
No cure, so too, though stream on stream should pour
Their swift-cleansing waters on the hand of blood, the old
Stain shall not be wiped away.

EP.

For me, the Gods drove the engines of fate
Against my city, from home they led me
A captive slave to dwell in bondage.
And so I must needs endure my masters'
Commandments, righteous or no, and hide
My bitter hatred; yet beneath my cloak I weep
With heart chilled in secret grief
To see the wanton state of those set over me.

ELECTRA: Bondswomen, ministrants to the royal house,
Since you are my companions in this act
Of intercession, what do you advise?
What shall I say to dedicate these gifts,
What prayer contrive to please a father's ear?
That I have brought them from a loving wife
To lord beloved, an offering from my mother?
No, that would be too shameless—then what else,
While on the tomb these holy oils are laid?

Or shall I speak the words appointed, saying,
'Bless those who send these garlands in thy honour
And give for good gifts goodly recompense'?
Or pour in silence without ceremony,
Even as he died, a draught for earth to drink,
As though to cast out scourings, then turn and fling
The vessel from me with averted eyes?
Such is the matter in which I ask of you
To share with me your counsel, as we share
Within these doors a common enemy.
Therefore, fear not nor hide your thoughts from me;
For Destiny as sure awaits the free
As those who serve perforce another's will.

CHORUS: Since you desire it, as one to whom this tomb
Is as an altar, I will speak my mind.

ELECTRA: Yes, speak as a worshipper at my father's grave.

CHORUS: Bless in the act all those who wish him well.

ELECTRA: Whom of my kinsfolk can I so entitle?

CHORUS: Yourself, and then Aegisthus' enemies.

ELECTRA: The prayer must be made then for you and me?

CHORUS: You understand; take thought accordingly.

ELECTRA: Who else can be joined to our company?

CHORUS: Orestes far away; forget him not.

ELECTRA: Well said: oh, that indeed is good advice.

CHORUS: Remember too those guilty of his blood.

ELECTRA: What shall I say? Instruct me in your meaning.

CHORUS: Ask him to grant that God or man shall come—

ELECTRA: Shall come to judge them, or to execute?

CHORUS: Yes, say quite plainly, to take life for life.

ELECTRA: Is that a righteous prayer to ask of heaven?

CHORUS: Why not?—to pray ill for your enemies.

ELECTRA: O messenger between the quick and dead,
Hermes, whose home is underground, convey
My prayers to the infernal Gods who watch
Over my father's house, to Earth who brings
All creatures forth, and having nurtured them
Is quickened by them and conceives again,
While I pour out this lustral offering
And call upon my father to have mercy
On me and lead Orestes back to shine
A light unto the house; who both are now
As outcasts, sold and bartered by our mother
For her new lord, Aegisthus, who with her
Stands guilty of thy murder—I a slave,
Orestes banished, disinherited,
And they the proud usurpers of thy labours.
Oh, I beseech thee, speed Orestes home—
That is my prayer—O hear it, father, hear,
And grant to me in heart more chastity,
In hand more cleanness, than my mother had.
So much for us, and for thy enemies
Vouchsafe to come with judgment on their sins,
From those who took life justly taking life.
This evil supplication, made for *them*,
I set amid my own petitions fair.
To us be giver of good gifts, by grace
Of Heaven and Earth and of triumphant Right!
So having prayed, I pour these offerings.
Your part it is to crown them with lament
And with loud voice make music for the dead.

CHORUS: Come and weep, let fall the plashing tear,
Fall for our fallen lord,

Before a tomb that shields the good
And holds pollution hence, with these
Propitiations paid. Hearken to us, O King;
O lord, stir thy ghostly sense, wake and hear!
Ototototoi!
Ah me, might he come, a warrior,
One who shall free the House, one with a Scythian bow
To bend afar off, and armed too with that
Bludgeon of wood to wield in close fight as well!

ELECTRA: Our gifts the Earth has drunk, my father taken.
And now I have strange news to share with you.

CHORUS: What is it? My heart throbs in the dance of fear.

ELECTRA: I found this shorn lock resting on the tomb.

CHORUS: Whose can it be? What man or maid has left it?

ELECTRA: So much is plain for all to understand.

CHORUS: I understand not. Teach your elders truth.

ELECTRA: None would have laid it there save only me.

CHORUS: True, those who should have mourned are enemies.

ELECTRA: And yet to look on it is very like.

CHORUS: To whose? Tell me; I miss your meaning still.

ELECTRA: My own; in semblance it is close to mine.

CHORUS: Orestes—can it be? A secret tribute?

ELECTRA: His hair was of this very quality.

CHORUS: But how could he have dared to bring it hither?

ELECTRA: He sent it maybe to grace his father's grave.

CHORUS: Why then, this news is greater cause for tears,
If in the land he never shall set foot.

ELECTRA: I too am stricken to the heart. The waves
Of sorrow swell and beat against my breast,
While from these thirsty eyes falls drop by drop
Unstaunched the surging tide, as I behold
These curls; for whom of all my countrymen
Can I account their owner, if not his?
Hers they could never be, the murderess,
My mother too, though how unmotherly
In spirit to her children, impious!
I know not how I can accept it thus,
A certain gift from him, my best-beloved,
Orestes; yet the hope still smiles on me.
Alas!
If only it could have spoken, a messenger
To calm my spirit tossed from doubt to doubt,
That I might know whether to cast it out
With loathing, shorn from some unloving head,
Or that being kin we might lament together
And grace this tomb with homage to our father!
The Gods whom I implore already know
The storm on which my helpless spirit drifts.
Yet, if it be ours to win deliverance,
From a small seed shall spring a mighty stem.
But look! Footprints—another testimony—
His own, and with them some companion's—
Two outlines are there here, two tracks of feet.
And see, the heels of these are like my own!
The impress of the instep measured out
Accords with mine and makes a perfect match.
What agony is here, what shattered wit!
(Orestes comes forward)

ORESTES: Thank God for the fulfilment of your prayer
And ask a blessing for what is yet to come.

ELECTRA: For what am I indebted to him now?

ORESTES: Behold the sight you have prayed so long to see.

ELECTRA: How do you know whom I have called upon?

ORESTES: I know Orestes is your idol still.

ELECTRA: And how have I been favoured in my prayer?

ORESTES: Here am I, and none dearer shall you find.

ELECTRA: Ah, stranger, 'tis a trick you play on me.

ORESTES: If so, I have conspired against myself.

ELECTRA: You wish to make a mock of my distress.

ORESTES: If I mock yours, I also mock my own.

ELECTRA: As being Orestes then, I say to you—

ORESTES: You see me here, and now you know me not.
Yet when you found that token of my tears,
And likewise when you followed up my tracks,
Your heart leapt at the fancied sight of me.
Compare that lock with those from whence 'twas cut,
Your brother's, of like measure to your own.
Look at this cloth—it is your handiwork:
See where your batten struck, and see the beasts
Which you designed in the embroidery.
Ah, calm yourself, restrain this burst of joy.
Our bitterest enemies are those most near.

ELECTRA: O happy presence, in this heart endowed
With fourfold portion: father art thou to me,
To thee is turned a mother's love, for she
Is hated utterly, and a sister's, whom
They killed without pity; and last for thee,
My own true brother, thine is all my love.

CHORUS: O darling of thy father's house, O hope
Watered with tears, seed of deliverance,
Trust in thy courage, and thou shalt repossess

Thy father's heritage, if only Might
And Right stand by thy side, and with them third,
Of all the greatest, Zeus Deliverer!

ORESTES: Zeus, Zeus, look down upon our state, regard
The eagle's offspring orphaned of their sire,
Whom the fell serpent folded in her coils
And crushed to death; for his bereaved are sore
Oppressed with hunger, lacking yet the strength
To bring the father's quarry to the nest.
And so we stand, my sister here and I,
Before thy face, a brood both robbed of sire,
Both fugitives from home. Our father, once
Thy priest, held thee in highest honour: so,
If thou destroy his nestlings, from what hand
So liberal shalt thou receive the gifts
Of festive sacrifice? If thou destroy
The eagle's brood, no more shalt thou have signs
To send from heaven, no more this royal stem,
This withered stump of greatness, will avail
To grace thy altar on the days appointed.
Oh, cherish it, restore it! Then this house,
That now seems fallen, shall once more be great.

CHORUS: O children, saviours of your father's house,
Hush, lest some eavesdropper with idle tongue
Make all known to our masters, whom may I
See burnt alive in pools of spluttering pitch!

ORESTES: Apollo will not break his faith, by whose
Almighty oracles I am commanded
To take on me this hazard. Loud and long
His prophetess predicted chilly blasts
Of pestilence to turn the heart's blood cold,
If I should fail to seek those murderers out
And put them to the death my father died,
Their lives for his, goaded to fury by

The heavy lash of disinheritance;
Or else the penalty, he said, would fall
On my own soul—a host of horrors, some
Sent up from earth by the resentful dead,
Which he named thus, ulcers to mount the flesh
With ravenous jaws and eat the substance up,
And out of them a crop of hoary hairs;
And worse, he told me of the fierce assault
Of Furies, sprung out of a father's blood.
Roused by petitionings of fallen kin,
The dusky weapon of infernal powers,
Madness and sudden panic in the night,
Doth haunt and harass, so he said, and scourge
The bruised and bleeding, execrated body
Out of the land; for such there is no part
In mixing of the wine, he may not pour
Drink-offerings at grace, his father's wrath
Unseen shall bar him from the altar, none
Shall give him welcome, none shall with him lodge—
Unhonoured, unbefriended, he shall waste
Lonely away to everlasting death.
Such were his oracles—shall I trust them not?
And, though I trust not, still it must be done.
Many desires all gather to one end—
The God's command, a son's grief for a father,
The pinch of hunger for my lost estate,
And anger that my glorious countrymen,
Whose valiant spirit captured Ilium,
Should be the subjects of two women; for
He has a woman's heart, as he shall see!

KOMMOS

CHORUS: O Fate Almighty, with favour of Zeus
Ordain that the end shall be set in the path
Where Righteousness walks into battle!

'For the tongue which hateth, let hatred of tongue
Be rendered!'—with these words Justice doth cry
In a loud voice claiming her payment:
'For a murderous blow let a murderous blow
Be struck.' Let the doer be done by!—so
In a saying of old it is ordered.

STR. I

ORESTES: Teach me, O father, O father dread,
How by word or action
To waft upward thy soul from where
Earth in her bosom keeps it.
As day is reversed in night, so doth a dirge of praises
Appear unto the slain of old
Pleasing and full of comfort.

STR. 2

CHORUS: My son, the flames devour the flesh but not the spirit.
The soul of the dead in time shows to the quick his anger;
For a dirge to those departed is a lamp to light the sinner,
And the just lament of children for the father who begot them
From full hearts shall be sent ahunting.

ANT. I

ELECTRA: Father, incline thine ear to this
Dirge of mournful numbers,
As each child doth address his own
Tribute of lamentation.
As suppliant I implore sanctuary, he as outcast.
We stand doomed to destruction—naught,
Naught is there here but evil.

CHORUS: And yet in his season shall God if he will
Set the voice to a happier tune: instead
Of a dirge at the tomb of the dead he shall raise
In the house of the king blithe music to greet
Good cheer in the flagon of friendship.

STR. 3

ORESTES: Would that in Ilium, father, felled by a Trojan lance,
In fight laid low, thy life had ended,
To leave a fair name at home behind thee,
To leave these thy children | to walk eyed of all men,
To rest in a sepulchre far, far away, and to sleep, a peaceful
Load for the House of Atreus!

ANT. 2

CHORUS: Then loving, dearly loved of all who fell in battle,
A regent among the dead, now wouldst thou reign in glory,
In attendance on the greatest of the lords who rule the darkness
(For in life thou wast a great king), and dispense the fate
of mortals
With dread sceptre of lasting judgment.

ANT. 3

ELECTRA: Ah, not a tomb in Troy, laid in dust with the rest
of those
That War struck down beneath her towers,
Beside the waters | of swift Scamander!
I wish rather those who destroyed him | had perished,
Destroyed by their own, and their downfall been told from
afar, before we
Tasted of tribulation!

CHORUS: Ah, that were a bliss more precious than gold,
My daughter, beyond
All price; but thy prayer is vain, for
With the beat of a scourge double-dealt is the blow
Struck home, one blow for the champion at rest
Long since in the earth, and another for those
Who have unclean hands, our masters—what crime
So abhorrent to son and to daughter?

STR. 4

ORESTES: That is a shot to the heart
Straight as a shaft from the bow.
Zeus, Zeus, from under the earth speed
Fatal revenge to follow
The foul hand of the mortal sinner,
Even a son that is like his mother!

STR. 5

CHORUS: May these lips soon be moved in song
To chant gladly the alleluia
Over a man and woman
Stricken to death! for why still
Hide the hope that is beating
Within me? The heart's front is battered
Down by the fierce gust of a long-rankling rage and bitter spite.

ANT. 4

ELECTRA: When will he strike with his hand,
Zeus, in the fulness of power,
Oh, when shall the head be sundered?
Grant that a sign be given!
A just payment I seek from sinners.
Hear me, O Earth and ye shades majestic!

CHORUS: Truly 'tis written that blood once shed
On the ground is athirst for the shedding of yet
More blood; foul murder is crying abroad
For a Fury to spring from the slaughtered and crown
One violent end with another.

STR. 6

ORESTES: Oh fie, Earth; shame, infernal sovranties!
Look on us, O ye mighty curses of the dead,
The seed of Atreus, a lonely remnant here,
Astray and lost, dispossessed
And homeless—O Zeus, shall naught avail us?

ANT. 5

CHORUS: And yet fear shakes my fainting heart
At these ominous cries of anguish.
Hopeless awhile, it groweth
Black to the core in darkest
Fear for the words they utter.
But when soon with strength armed for action
Courage returns, then is despair banished, joy again prevails.

ANT. 6

ELECTRA: With what words might | our purpose best be won?
Is it the wrongs I bore at those motherly hands?
The tongue shall speak soft, but those are unassuaged;
For like the fierce wolf my heart
Is true to hers, deaf to all beguilement.

STR. 7

CHORUS: I beat my breast and danced an eastern dirge,
And like a Cissian mourner mad
With clutching hands, with rending nails,
On breast and cheek I mingled tears with blood.
And up and down again the rapid rain of blows
Did beat on these brows in tune with loud lament.

ELECTRA: Oh me, hateful heart,
Oh wicked mother! hateful was his bearing-out,
A king, without followers,
With none to mourn over him,
Thou laidst him unwept in earth unhallowed.

STR. 8

ORESTES: Ah, can it be? So dishonoured! Ah me,
For those dishonours she shall repay him,
With help of almighty powers,
With stroke of these hands of mine.
Let her but die, then let me be taken!

ANT. 8

CHORUS: His limbs were lopped first—thou shalt be told all,—
Cut off by those hands that thus entombed him.
She sought by such means to load
Thy days with grief past compare.
And so he lies, buried in dishonour.

ANT. 7

ELECTRA: Such was my father's death, and I was kept
Dishonoured, deemed of no account,
Within my chamber kennelled like a dog,
With tears outstripping laughter in my eyes
In secret streams of solitary grief.
Remember all this, and write it in thy heart.

CHORUS: Through unsealèd ear
Let sink the truth to still and steady sense.
For so the case standeth now,
But more the heart yearns to hear.
With calm resolve must | the lists be entered.

STR. 9

ORESTES: I call on thee, father, fight beside thine own!

ELECTRA: And I to his join a sorrowful complaint.

CHORUS: And all with one voice together cry aloud,
O hear us, rise from darkness, wake,
Stand by our side for battle!

ANT. 9

ORESTES: With Strife shall Strife join in battle, Right with Right.

ELECTRA: O heaven, hear, grant our task a just event!

CHORUS: A shudder steals through my soul to hear them pray.
The fatal end has long been fixed,
Now it is near fulfilment.

STR. 10

Evil inborn and bred,
Terrible stroke of bloodshed
Chanted to tunes of ruin!
O grief, grief that defies endurance,
O pain, pain that is past appeasement!

ANT. 10

Cure for the House is none
Save of itself; its own true
Kindred alone can heal it
In fell strife of avenging bloodshed.
We sing this to the powers of darkness.

Blest lords of the dead, lend ear unto this
Intercession, and graciously send unto these
Two children the strength that shall conquer!

ORESTES: Father, who died a most unkingly death,
Bequeath to us the sovranty of thy house!

ELECTRA: And I entreat thee, father, make me free,
Who now am sold in slavery to Aegisthus.

ORESTES: And so thou shalt receive the solemn feasts
By ancient custom ordered: else the rich
Meats of the buried dead shall be denied thee.

ELECTRA: Out of my dowry I shall bring thee gifts
Upon my wedding-day, and in my heart
Thy tomb shall ever hold the place of honour.

ORESTES: Earth, send my father to look upon the battle!

ELECTRA: Persephone, release his shining might!

ORESTES: Father, remember the bath that was thy death!

ELECTRA: Remember the strange net they spread for thee!

ORESTES: And snared thy limbs in fetters of fine thread!

ELECTRA: Ignobly trapped in cunning coverlets!

ORESTES: Father, do these reproaches stir thee not?

ELECTRA: Lift up to us that countenance beloved!

ORESTES: Send Justice to do battle for thine own,
Or grant that we get the like grip of them,
If thou wouldst vanquish those who vanquished thee!

ELECTRA: Give ear to one last cry: regard us here,
Thy son and daughter, nestlings clustered round
Thy tomb, and have compassion on our tears!

ORESTES: Let not the seed of Pelops wholly perish;
For so, in spite of death, thou art not dead!

ELECTRA: Children are saving voices of remembrance
Which tie the dead to life, as floats that draw
The drag-net safe out of the vasty deep.

ORESTES: Hear us; for thy sake have we cried to thee.
Grant our entreaty and so save thyself!

CHORUS: These orisons have been commensurate
To recompense a long-neglected grave.
Now, since thy spirit is resolved to act,
'Tis time to put thy fortune to the proof.

ORESTES: So shall it be; but first 'tis not amiss
To ask what prompted her to dedicate
These offerings at the tomb, what afterthought
Of tardy penance for a sin past cure?—
Not goodwill to the dead; for such a gift
Could earn no thanks nor cancel the offence.
A world of offerings bestowed on blood
Once shed were labour wasted, so 'tis said.
Can you instruct me in what she intended?

CHORUS: I can, for I was with her. The wicked woman
Has sent these gifts because her heart was tossed
In dreams and rambling terrors of the night.

ORESTES: Did she declare the nature of her vision?

CHORUS: She said she dreamed to her was born a snake.

ORESTES: What followed then? how did her story end?

CHORUS: She nursed it like a child in swaddling-clothes.

ORESTES: What nurture did it crave—a new-born serpent?

CHORUS: She dreamed she gave it breast and suckled it.

ORESTES: With paps unwounded by so vile a thing?

CHORUS: Amidst her milk it drew a curd of blood.

ORESTES: Ah, this should be no idle apparition.

CHORUS: Then with a shriek of terror she awoke;
The lamps whose eyes were closed throughout the house
At her command flared up, and then she sent
These offerings in hope of surgery
To heal the deep affliction of her spirit.

ORESTES: I pray this Earth, I pray my father's tomb,
That this vision may prove oracular.
As I interpret it, it tallies well.
Since, issuing from whence I saw the light,
The serpent-child was wrapt in swaddling-clothes,
And since it mouthed the breast that nourished me,
With kindly milk mingling a curd of blood,
Whereat she cried in terror, it must be
That, even as she gave that monster life,
So she must die a violent death, and I,
The dragon of her dream, shall murder her.

CHORUS: Your reading of the portent I accept:
So be it. Now instruct your followers
What they must do and what forbear to do.

ORESTES: 'Tis simply told. First, *she* must go within
And keep our covenant from all concealed,
That they whose cunning caught and killed a king

Be caught themselves by cunning in the trap
They laid for him, as Loxias commands,
The Lord Apollo, prophet ever true.
Then I, apparelled as a stranger, girt
With gear of travel, shall approach the door
With Pylades, my true confederate,
Affecting speech Parnassian, mimicking
The Phocian voice and accent; then, if no
Doorkeeper come to bid us welcome, since
It is a house bewitched with sin, we'll wait
Till passers-by take stock of us and say,
'Where is Aegisthus? is he not at home?
If he has been informed, why does he keep
The palace closed against petitioners?'
And, once across the threshold, if I find
That miscreant seated on my father's throne,
Or if he come to greet me and uplift
Those eyes, which soon, I swear, shall be cast down,
Before he ask, 'Where is the stranger from?'
My steel shall strike and make a corpse of him,
And so a Fury never starved of slaughter
Shall drain her third draught of unmingled blood.
Meanwhile, to *you* I say, keep watch within
That all may fall out true to our design.
To *you* a tongue well-guarded I commend,
Silence in season and timeliness in speech.
The rest is for my comrade's eyes alone,
To guide me in this contest of the sword.
(Orestes and Pylades withdraw; Electra goes into the palace)

STR. I FIRST STASIMON

Fearful beasts numberless,
Strange and hurtful, breed on earth;
Monsters foul swim the deep; teeming seas
Clasp them close; and baleful lights sweeping through the
vaulted skies

Hang disastrous over all
Creatures that fly and that creep on the ground; and remember
How they rage, the stormy blasts.

ANT. I

Yet the works dared by man's
Froward spirit who shall tell?
Woman too, whose perverse loves devise
Crimes of blood, provoking bloodstained revenges, sin for sin;
Once a woman's lawless lust
Gains the supremacy, swiftly it leads to destruction
Wedded ties in beast and man.

STR. 2

Those who be not fully fledged of wit,
Thus shall learn: let them
Take thought touching that
Flash of torch-lit treachery,
Which the hard heart of Althaea plotted,
By whose hand the firebrand was burnt which
Dated back to the day her son
Cried as he issued from her
Womb, and measured his span of life
On to the death appointed.

ANT. 2

No less hateful too was Scylla, that
Wicked daughter, whose
False heart foe-beguiled
Dared the death of dearest kin,
All for one necklace rare, wrought of fine gold,
A gift out of Crete: hence in secret,
While in slumber her Nisus lay,
Ah, she shore his immortal
Locks—a pitiless heart was hers!
Hermes led him to darkness.

STR. 3

And since I call back to mind the wicked crimes
Of old . . .—To no purpose! *This* unhallowed, vile
Union, which the house abhors,
A wife's deceit framed against a warrior,
Against her true-wedded lord—
Do you with disloyal heart approve of that?
I praise the hearth where no fires of passion burn,
A meek heart such as graces woman.

ANT. 3

—Of all the crimes told in tales the Lemnian
Is chief, a sin cried throughout the world with such
Horror that, if men relate
Some monstrous outrage, they call it Lemnian.
Abhorred of man, scorned of God,
Their seed is cast out, uprooted evermore;
For none respects what the Gods abominate.
Is *this* not well and justly spoken?

STR. 4

A sword of piercing steel is poised
To strike well home, which unerring Justice
Shall thrust to cleave the hearts of all
Those who trample underfoot
The sanctities
Of Zeus, to ungodly deeds inclining.

ANT. 4

The stem of Justice standeth firm,
And Fate's strong hand forgeth steel to arm her.
There comes to wipe away with fresh
Blood the blood of old a son,
Obeying some
Inscrutable | Fury's deadly purpose.

(Enter Orestes and Pylades. They go up to the door)

ORESTES: Ho there, ho! Hear me, open to my knocking!
Ho, who is there? Ho, who is at home?
I call a third time for some answering step,
If Aegisthus permits the house to grant
Strangers their due of hospitality.
(A servant comes to the door)

SERVANT: All right, I hear you! Where is the stranger from?

ORESTES: Announce me to the masters of the house.
My mission is to them—I bring them news.
Go quickly, for Night's dusky chariot
Draws on apace the time for travellers
To moor beneath some hospitable roof.
Let someone in authority come forth,
A woman, or more fittingly a man;
For then our converse need not wear the veil
Of modesty—man freely speaks with man
And in a sentence makes his purpose plain.
(Clytemnestra appears at the door, attended by Electra)

CLYTEMNESTRA: Strangers, declare your wishes. You shall have
Such entertainment as befits this house—
Warm baths, a bed to ease limbs travel-tired,
And presence of an honest company;
But if you have in hand some graver matter,
That is man's work, to whom we shall impart it.

ORESTES: I am a stranger out of Phocis, come
To Argos on an errand of my own.
Scarce had I set my feet upon the road,
When, meeting with a man unknown to me—
Strophius the Phocian was his name, he said,—
'Stranger', said he to me, 'if you are bound
For Argos, please convey from me this message:
Inform his parents that their son, Orestes,
Is dead, and bring me answer back again,
Whether his people wish to take him home

Or leave him buried in a foreign land,
For evermore an exile. Meanwhile the round
Ribs of a brazen urn enclose the dust
Of one whose death has had its meed of tears.'
That is the message, though whether I address
One in authority and near to him,
I know not, but his parents should be told.

ELECTRA: Oh, all is gone, all pitilessly despoiled!
O Curse of this sad House, unconquerable,
How wide thy vision! Even that which seemed
Well-ordered, safe beyond the reach of harm,
Thou hast brought down with arrows from afar,
And left me desolate, stripped of all I loved.
And now Orestes—he who wisely thought
To keep his foot outside the miry clay,
Now that one hope prophetic which might yet
Have healed at last the wicked masquerade
Within this palace, mark it not as present.

ORESTES: I could have wished, on coming to a house
So blest of heaven, that happy news had made
Me known to you and welcome; for what can be
So kindly as the sweet communion
Of host and stranger? Yet my judgment would
Have counted it a sin not to perform
So grave an office for those dear to me
According to my word and plighted vow.

CLYTEMNESTRA: Nay, all that you deserve you shall be given.
Your news still leaves you welcome, for, if you
Had not conveyed it, others would have come.
And now it is the hour for travellers
To be attended after the long day's road.
(To Electra) Escort him into the men's chambers, with
His follower and companion of the way,
And let their persons there be duly tended.

Do this, I say, as you shall answer for it.
We shall inform the master of the house,
And then, with friends in plenty, we shall take
Counsel together touching this event.
(Clytemnestra, Electra, Orestes and Pylades go into the palace)

CHORUS: Handmaids of the house all faithful and true,
O when shall we lift
Our voices in praise of Orestes?
O hear, mother Earth, O tomb of the dead,
Who hidest the dust of a monarch-at-arms,
Answer us now, now send us thy power;
For the hour is at hand for Temptation to bring
Her deceits to the fray, for the God of the dead,
Hermes, to appear from the darkness and watch
This duel of sword and of slaughter.
(The Nurse comes out of the palace)

This stranger, it would seem, is making mischief.
Here is Orestes' old nurse, bathed in tears.
What brings you here, Cilissa, to the gates
With grief for your unchartered company?

NURSE: My mistress has commanded me to bring
Aegisthus to the strangers instantly,
That he may hear their message man from man.
Before the servants she assumes a set
And sorrowful aspect, but in her eyes
There lurks a smile for what has come to pass
For her so happily, though for this house
The strangers' news means misery evermore.
And sure *his* heart will be uplifted too
To hear that message. Oh my heavy grief,
How many bitter agonies of old
And all confused this breast of mine has borne
Within these walls of Atreus, and yet none,
No sorrow so insufferable as this!

All else I bore with patiently, but now
My dear Orestes, my life's long loving care,
Entrusted from his mother's arms to mine,
Breaking my sleep with many a summons shrill,
With daily troubles multiplied in vain:
For sure, a witless babe, like a dumb beast,
Must needs have nurse's wit to nourish it.
A child in swaddling-clothes cannot declare
His wants, that he would eat, or drink, or make
Water, and childish bellies will not wait
Upon attendance. Of all this prophetess,
And often falsified—a laundress then
To wash the linen shining-white again,
Fuller and nurse set on a common task—
Such was the double trade I plied, as I
Nursed young Orestes, his father's son and heir.
And now, alas, they tell me he is dead,
And I must take to him whose wickedness
Infects the house news that will make him glad.

CHORUS: With what equipment does she bid him come?

NURSE: Equipment? why? I do not understand.

CHORUS: Attended by his retinue, or alone?

NURSE: She bids him bring his royal bodyguard.

CHORUS: Then, since you hate him, not a word of that.
Tell him to come alone, and quickly too,
With naught to fear, and hear with gladdened heart.

NURSE: What, are you friendly to this present news?

CHORUS: Who knows but Zeus may turn an ill-wind yet?

NURSE: How, if Orestes, our last hope, is gone?

CHORUS: Not so would a good prophet read it yet.

NURSE: Ah, have you heard some contrary report?

CHORUS: Go, take your message, do as you are bid.
The Gods will care for that which is their care.

NURSE: I go and will obey you. May the Gods
Grant that all this shall end in what is best!
(Exit)

STR. 1

SECOND STASIMON

Now, I pray, lend us ear, Father Zeus,
Lord of high Olympus, vouch-
Safe success unto all those that seek
The rule of chaste wisdom enthroned again!
Naught have I asked of thee
But what is just: Zeus, I pray, defend us!
Ah, let the champion
Who hath gone in be upheld, Zeus,
In the fray. Thou, who hast made him
Great, shalt take at will
A twofold recompense and threefold.

ANT. 1

Think of that sire beloved whose bereft
Colt is yoked to sorrow's car.
He who keeps measured pace most is like
To see sustained steady and even step
On till the long race is run,
Sped with feet surely striding forward.
Ah, let the champion
Who hath gone in be upheld, Zeus,
In the fray. Thou, who hast made him
Great, shalt take at will
A twofold recompense and threefold.

STR. 2

Deities who dwell within,
Glad of heart, arbiters of royal wealth,
Hearken kindly to our prayer,

So with vengeance new redeem
The full debt of bloody deeds of yore.
No more let old murder breed and multiply.
God of the great cavern in glory established,
Let us rejoice, and set a crown on the palace;
Oh, let it swiftly appear,
Gleaming and friendly and free
Out of the veil of encircling darkness!

ANT. 2

Justly may he join with us,
Maia's son, named the keen and cunning one;
Much at will he can reveal,
Night he draws dim and dark before the eye,
With voice veiled that none may understand,
Nor yet by day plainer doth his form appear.
God of the great cavern in glory established,
Let us rejoice, and set a crown on the palace;
Oh, let it swiftly appear,
Gleaming and friendly and free
Out of the veil of encircling darkness!

STR. 3

Thus at last, after this
House hath found deliverance,
Music set to breezes fair,
Women's shrill songs of joy
Shall be heard, the wizard's chant:
'Well she sails!
Mine the gain, mine, as trouble draws aside,
Bringing peace to those I love.'
And with stout heart as the time comes
For the act, cry to her, 'Father!' as thy answer
Unto her cry of 'Child!'
And so slay in blameless bloodshed.

ANT. 3

Keep within thy breast a heart
Strong as Perseus', bring to all
Those that love thee, some that lie
Under earth, some above,
Joy of glad deliverance.
Make the end
Bloody, and wipe out at last the guilty seed,
Wipe it out for evermore!
And with stout heart as the time comes
For the act, cry to her, 'Father!' as thy answer
Unto her cry of 'Child!'
And so slay in blameless bloodshed.

(Enter Aegisthus)

AEGISTHUS: I come in answer to the summoner.
They tell me of some news that has been brought
By strangers, tidings most unwelcome to us,
Orestes' death, another stroke of grief
To open ancient sores in this sad house,
Already maimed and stricken to the core.
How shall I judge whether it be the truth
Or woman's idle talk, by terror set
Aflame and soaring, and no death at all?
What proof have you of this to reason plain?

CHORUS: We heard the news; but go within and ask
The strangers. Mere report is little worth
When a man can make inquiry on the spot.

AEGISTHUS: I want to see that messenger and ask
If he was present at the death himself
Or from faint rumour heard an empty tale.
I'll not be hoodwinked: my wits are not asleep.

(Aegisthus goes into the palace)

CHORUS: Zeus, what shall I say, where rightly begin
With a prayer and a cry to thy name, and in true
Loyalty make this
My address to befit the occasion?
Yes, now the essay of the murderous blade
Is about to set over the house of the lord
Agamemnon destruction for ever;
Or if not, with the splendour of torches ablaze
For his freedom regained shall the son be enthroned
In the land of his sires
And recover the wealth of his fathers.
So much is at issue, and single he goes,
The heroic Orestes, and twain are his foes;
O grant that he goeth to conquer!

(A cry from Aegisthus within)

Oh!
How is this? How does all go within?
The work's afoot. Let us stand apart awhile,
That we be counted innocent of harm.
The issue of the battle has been sealed.

(The Servant comes to the door)

SERVANT: Grief, utter grief! My master is struck down.
Oh heavy grief—a third cry for the dead!
Aegisthus is no more. Come, open quick!
Unbolt the women's chambers! A strong hand too
It needs—though not indeed to help the dead.
Ho!
Ah, they are deaf or sleeping, and my cries
Are wasted. What is Clytemnestra doing?
Where is she? Now at last, it seems, her neck
Shall touch the block beneath the axe of Justice.

(Clytemnestra comes to the door)

CLYTEMNESTRA: What is it? What is the meaning of that shout?

SERVANT: It means the living are being killed by the dead.

CLYTEMNESTRA: Ah me, a riddle! yet I read its meaning.
We killed by cunning and by cunning die.
Quick, let me have a man-axe! let us see
Who wins, who loses! It has come to this.
(Orestes and Pylades come out of the palace)

ORESTES: I want you. As for him, it is well enough.

CLYTEMNESTRA: Aegisthus, dearest lord! Oh, he is dead!

ORESTES: You love him? Well then, you shall share his grave,
In all things faithful, even unto death.

CLYTEMNESTRA: O stay, my son! Dear child, have pity on
This bosom where in slumber long ago
Your toothless gums drew in the milk of life.

ORESTES: Pylades, what shall I do? shall I have mercy?

PYLADES: What then hereafter of the oracles
And solemn covenants of Loxias?
Let all men hate thee rather than the Gods.

ORESTES: That is good counsel—your word shall prevail.
Come with me—I mean to kill you by his side.
While he lived, you preferred him to my father;
So sleep in death beside him, since you loved
Him, and hated whom you should have loved.

CLYTEMNESTRA: I brought you up—with you I would grow old.

ORESTES: What, dwell with me, my father's murderess?

CLYTEMNESTRA: Fate was a partner to his death, my child.

ORESTES: And that same fate has now decreed your own.

CLYTEMNESTRA: Have you no dread, my child, of a mother's curse?

ORESTES: Your child indeed, until you cast me out.

CLYTEMNESTRA: No, not cast out—I sent you away to friends.

ORESTES: Yes, the son of a royal father, foully sold.

CLYTEMNESTRA: What was the payment that I took for you?

ORESTES: I cannot answer that—for very shame.

CLYTEMNESTRA: No, no—remember too *his* wantonness!

ORESTES: Accuse him not—for you he toiled abroad.

CLYTEMNESTRA: It is hard for a woman parted from her man.

ORESTES: What but his labour keeps her safe at home?

CLYTEMNESTRA: So then, my son, you mean to kill
your mother?

ORESTES: It is not I, it is you who kill yourself.

CLYTEMNESTRA: Beware the hell-hounds of a mother's curse!

ORESTES: And how, if I spared you, escape from his?

CLYTEMNESTRA: My pleas are vain—warm tears on a cold tomb.

ORESTES: My father's destiny has determined yours.

CLYTEMNESTRA: Ah me, I bore a serpent, not a son.

ORESTES: That fearful vision was indeed prophetic.
Wrong shall be done you for the wrong you did.

(They go into the palace)

CHORUS: I weep for both and for their double pain.
Yet, since the tale of plenteous blood is crowned
In brave Orestes, I choose to have it so,
In order that the eye of this great house
May rise again, not perish utterly.

STR. I

THIRD STASIMON

Unto the sons of Priam Justice did come in time,
Heavy and harsh judgment;

To Agamemnon too and to his house it came,
A double lion, double strife.
Unto the uttermost he held his course heaven-sped,
Following well the Lord Apollo's command.
  Cry alleluia, lift up in the house a song,
  Deliverance from ill and from the waste of wealth
  By the unholy sinners twain,
  From rough thorny ways.

ANT. I

And he hath come, the God who with a sly assault
Waiteth to work judgment;
Yea, and his hand was guided in the battle by
The child of Zeus begotten-true,
Whom it is right and meet that mortals name Righteousness.
Deadly the blast she breathes on all evildoers!
  Cry alleluia, lift up in the house a song,
  Deliverance from ill and from the waste of wealth
  By the unholy sinners twain,
  From rough thorny ways.

STR. 2

Even as Loxias on Parnassus cried
Out of his holy shrine, so doth his will advance
Never at fault against
The ingrown disease which in the house is lodged.
For Godhead doth e'er prevail over sin
With sure surgery.
Worthy of praise the all-supreme power divine.
  On us the light hath shined, now is the bridle-bit
  Lifted from out the house.
  Gladly, O House, arise! for it was long enough
  The curb of sin did hold thee down.

ANT. 2

Soon shall the feet of Time Perfecter enter in,
In at the royal gates, when he hath cleansed the hearth

Of the defiling sin.
With clean flow of bloodshed he shall purify.
With kind fortune couched and fair-eyed to see
For all who have wept
Shall aliens within be laid low again.
On us the light hath shined, now is the bridle-bit
Lifted from out the house.
Gladly, O House, arise! for it was long enough
The curb of sin did hold thee down.

(The doors are opened and torches are alight within, revealing the bodies of Aegisthus and Clytemnestra wrapped in purple robes and laid upon a couch, Orestes standing over them)

ORESTES: Behold our country's double tyranny,
The murderous pillagers of my father's house,
How stately once they sat upon their thrones,
And now how loving, as their condition shows,
They lie, still faithful to their plighted vows,
Both pledged to slay my father, likewise pledged
To die themselves together—they kept their word.
And you who hear of these calamities,
Behold the snare which they contrived to knot
About my hapless father's hands and feet.
What name becomes it, though I choose the best?
A pit for beasts, a winding-sheet to catch
A dead man's legs? or would you rather say
A net, or sweeping cloak that trips the heels,
Trick of some crafty highwayman who lives
On silver plundered from the traveller?
With such an equipage how many lives
He would waylay, how it would warm his heart!
Come, spread it out, stand round it in a ring,
This cunning coverlet, that he who is
Of all created father and looks down
On the whole world, the Sun, having beheld
My mother's wicked handiwork, may stand

My witness in the judgment yet to come,
And certify that I have sought her death
Justly—as for Aegisthus, he has paid
The price prescribed for all adulterous lechers;
But she, who planned this horror for her own
Master, to whom within the womb she once
Bore offspring, then a load of love, but now,
As shown by its sharp fangs, of deadly hate,
What do you think of her? If she had been
Some scorpion or sea-serpent, her very touch,
For sheer iniquity and wicked spirit,
Would breed corruption in the unbitten hand.
May such as she not share my house, but rather
May heaven destroy me and my seed for ever!

CHORUS: Ah me, how dread was the work of thy hands,
How fearful the death that befell thee!
In the fulness of time
Retribution bursts into blossom.

ORESTES: Was the deed hers or not? I have a witness,
This robe, that here she plunged Aegisthus' sword;
For bloodstains have conspired with time to wear
Much of the dye out of the threaded pattern.
Now I am here to speak my father's praises,
Now, only now, to make my lamentations.
And as I greet this web that wove his death,
I weep for all things done and suffered here,
For the whole race, and weep for my own fate,
Marked with the stains of this sad victory.

CHORUS: No man upon earth shall be brought to the end
Of his days unwounded by sorrow.
Distress is for some
Here present, for others abides yet.

ORESTES: So then, to tell you plainly,—I know not what
My end will be—my wits are out of hand,

Like horses that with victory in sight
Stampede out of the course, and in my heart,
As fear strikes up her tune, the dance begins,—
But, while I have my senses, I declare
To all my friends that I have killed my mother
In a just cause, my father's murderess,
A thing unclean, an execrable pest;
And to that desperate act my heart was lured
By homage to Apollo, who proclaimed
That, if I did this thing, I should be clear
Of guilt; if not,—I will not name the price,
Horrors beyond the furthest shaft of wit.
And now behold me as I turn my steps,
With boughs of supplication garlanded,
Unto the midmost shrine of Loxias
And glorious light of his undying fire,
An exile stained with kindred blood; for he
Commanded me to seek no hearth but his.
And all my countrymen I call to give
In time to come their witness, how these things
Were brought to pass—meanwhile, a wanderer,
An outcast from my country, I commend
Into their charge, in life and death, my name.

CHORUS: Thou hast done well, bend not thy lips to such
Ill-omened sayings and wild talk of woe.
Thou art deliverer of the land of Argos,
With one light stroke lopping two dragons' heads.

ORESTES: Ah!
What are those women? See them, Gorgon-like,
All clad in sable and entwined with coils
Of writhing snakes! Oh away, away!

CHORUS: What are these fancies, father's dearest son,
That fright thee? Stay and fear not. Thou hast won.

ORESTES: To me they are no fancies—only too clear—
Can you not see them?—hounds of a mother's curse!

CHORUS: Fresh is the bloodshed yet upon thy hands:
That is what brings confusion on thy wits.

ORESTES: O Lord Apollo, see how thick they come,
And from their eyes are dripping gouts of blood!

CHORUS: Thou shalt be purified! Apollo's touch
From these disasters shall deliver thee!

ORESTES: You cannot see them—look, how clear they are!
They come to hunt me down! Away, away!
(Exit Orestes)

CHORUS: Fortune attend thee, may God graciously
Watch over thee and guide thee to the end!

On the house of the king with a turbulent blast
Has the third storm broke
And expended hath swept to its ending.
First came the unmerciful slaughter of babes
And the feast on their flesh;
Next followed the fall of a king, in the bath
Struck down, the Achaean commander who led
All Greece into war;
And the third now present is saviour—or else
Is destruction his name?
O when shall the end come, where shall the rage
Of calamity sink into slumber?

EUMENIDES

CHARACTERS

ORESTES
GHOST OF CLYTEMNESTRA
APOLLO
HERMES
ATHENA
A PRIESTESS
CHORUS

EUMENIDES

(Before the temple of Apollo at Delphi. Enter the Priestess)

PRIESTESS: Chief of the Gods in prayer I venerate,
The first of prophets, Earth; and next to her
Themis, who from her mother, it is said,
Received the seat oracular; and the third,
Another child of Earth, the Titan maid
Phoebe, with free consent here found a home;
And she bestowed it as a birthday gift
On Phoebus, with it lending him her name.
The lakes and rocks of Delos he forsook,
And setting foot on Pallas' harboured shores
Came hither to Parnassus, on his way
Attended with all honour by the Sons
Of Hephaestus, who built a road for him
And tamed the wilderness before his feet.
And when he came, the people worshipped him
Under king Delphus, their lord and governor;
And Zeus, having inspired him with his art,
Set him, the fourth of prophets, on this throne,
Whence he is called Interpreter of Zeus,
Whose son he is, prophetic Loxias.
These Gods then are the preface to my prayers,
And with them I render the homage due
To Pallas of the Precinct, and likewise
The nymphs whose dwelling is the cavernous cliff
Corycian, home of birds and haunt beloved
Of spirits, the region held by Bromius
(This have I not forgotten) when he led
His Bacchants into battle and devised
The death of Pentheus like a hunted hare.

So, calling also on Poseidon's power,
Upon the springs of Pleistus, and last of all
On Zeus the Highest, Zeus the Perfecter,
I take my seat on the throne of prophecy.
And may this entry be more blest of them
Than any heretofore! Let Greeks approach
In the accustomed order of the lot;
As the God dictates, so shall I prophesy.

(She enters the temple, utters a loud cry, and returns)

Oh horror, horror to utter and behold,
Has driven me back from the house of Loxias;
Strengthless, with dragging step, upon my hands
I run. An aged woman terror-struck
Is nothing, or at most a child again.
I made my way into the laurelled shrine
And at the navel-stone I saw a man,
Defiled with murder, in suppliant posture, red
Blood dripping from the hands that grasped a sword
Fresh from the scabbard and a topmost branch
Of olive humbly garlanded with wool,
A fleece all silver-white. So much was plain;
But all around, asleep upon the thrones,
Lay a strange company of women—yet
Not women, Gorgons rather; nor again
To Gorgons can I liken them, for those
I saw once in a picture, plundering
The feast of Phineus; but no wings have these,
Yet black and utterly abominable,
Snoring in blasts that none may venture near,
With eyes that run with drops of loathsome rheum,
In raiment clad which it were a sin to bring
Near images of the Gods or roofs of men.
The tribe to which these visitants belong
I never saw, nor know what land could boast
Of such a brood and not repent her pangs.

As for the rest, let him take thought for it
Who owns the house, almighty Loxias,
Prophet and Healer, Interpreter of signs,
Himself of other houses Purifier.

(The interior of the temple is revealed, as described; with Apollo and Hermes standing behind Orestes)

APOLLO: I will keep faith, at watch continually,
Close at thy side and vigilant from afar,
And never gentle to thy enemies.
And now thou seest them here in slumber seized,
These ravenous monsters, stretched upon the ground,
Maidens abominable, children gray with years,
With whom no God consorts, nor man nor beast,
Abhorred alike in heaven and on earth,
For evil born, even as the darkness where
They dwell is evil, the abyss of Tartarus.
Yet thou must fly and grow not faint of heart.
They will track down thy steps from shore to shore,
For ever travelling the wide ways of earth
Past island cities, over distant seas,
And nurse thy tribulation patiently
Until thou comest to the citadel
Of Pallas, where in supplication clasp
Her antique image in thine arms; for there,
With judgment of thy suit and gentle charms
Of speech, we shall find out at last a way
From all these evils to deliver thee,
Being moved by me even to kill thy mother.

ORESTES: O Lord Apollo, thou knowest what is just,
And since thou knowest, O neglect it not!
Thy strength to do good lacks no warranty.

APOLLO: Remember, let thy heart not yield to fear.
And thou, my brother begotten of one sire,
True to thy name, go with him, guide the feet

Of this my suppliant; for the sanctity
Of outcasts from mankind, who take the road
With guidance fair, is sacred unto Zeus.
(Hermes and Orestes go. Enter the Ghost of Clytemnestra)

CLYTEMNESTRA: Oho! asleep! What good are you asleep?
And I, whom you dishonour, am reproached
Among the other dead unceasingly,
Hissed and cast out, homeless, a murderess!
I tell you they malign me shamefully,
While I, so cruelly treated by my own,
Slaughtered myself with matricidal hands,
No deity is indignant for my sake.
O let your conscience look upon these scars!
Remember all those sober blandishments,
Those wineless offerings which you have drunk,
Those sacrificial suppers on the hearth
At many a solemn midnight, which you shared
With none of heaven's deities: and now
All that is rudely trampled in the dust.
And *he* is gone: light as a fawn he sped
Out of the inmost meshes of your snare
And leapt away, and now he scoffs at you.
O hear as I plead with you for my soul!
O Goddesses of the underworld, awake!
I, Clytemnestra, call you now in dreams!

CHORUS: Mu, mu!

CLYTEMNESTRA: Ah, you may mew, but he is fled and gone;
For he has friends far different from mine.

CHORUS: Mu, mu!

CLYTEMNESTRA: Still slumbering and still compassionless!
The matricide, Orestes, has escaped!

CHORUS: Oh, oh!

CLYTEMNESTRA: Still whining in your drowsiness! Arise!
To do evil is your appointed task.

CHORUS: Oh, oh!

CLYTEMNESTRA: How sleep and weariness, strong confederates,
Have disenvenomed the fell dragon's rage!

CHORUS: Oh, oh! Find the scent, mark him down!

CLYTEMNESTRA: Though you give tongue like an unerring hound,
You chase the quarry only through your dreams.—
What are you doing? Rise, cast off fatigue!
Let not sleep soothe remembrance of your hurt!—
Let your heart ache with pangs of just reproach,
Which harry a good conscience like a scourge!—
Come, blow about his head your bloody breath,
Consume his flesh with blasts of bellied fire!
On, on, renew the hunt and wear him down! *(Exit)*

PARODOS

CHORUS: Awake, awake her there as I wake thee!
Still sleeping? Rise, cast slumber underfoot!
Let us see whether our enchantment works.

STR. I

Alas, alas, for shame! What have we suffered, friends!
Ah, suffered bitterly, and all in vain!
Suffered a fearful hurt, horrible! Oh the pain
Beyond strength to bear!
The game has leapt out of the snare and gone.
In slumber laid low, I let slip the prey.

ANT. I

Aha, son of Zeus, pilferer, pillager!
A youth to trample ancient deities,
Honouring such a suppliant abhorred of God,
An unfilial son!

A God, to steal away the matricide!
O who denies this was unjustly done?

STR. 2
In dream there came to me a dread reproach,
A blow such as might descend from some
Charioteer's stout hand,
Under the ribs, under the flank.
It rankles yet, red and sore,
Chill as frost, like the fell
Assault of public scourger's lash.

ANT. 2
This is the doing of the younger Gods,
Who transgress the powers appointed them.
Dripping with death, red drops
Cover the heel, cover the head.
Behold the Earth's central stone
Black with big stains of blood,
Possessed of vast pollution vile.

STR. 3
A prophet he, his own prophetic cell
He has himself profaned.
His was the act, the asking,
Honouring mortal things, reckless of laws divine
And dealing death to Fates born of old.

ANT. 3
He injures me, yet *him* he shall not free,
Not in the depths of hell,
Ne'er shall he be delivered.
Suppliant unabsolved, soon shall he find his brow
Defiled again with guilt thrice as great.

APOLLO: Out, out, I say, begone! I bid you leave
This mantic cell of your vile presence free;
Or soon a silver scorpion taking wing

From golden bow shall lay on you such smart
That from your swollen bellies you shall retch
The clotted blood from human bodies sucked.
No house is this to be approached by you,
But rather go where heads fall from the block,
Where eyes are gouged, throats slit, and boyhood's bloom
Blasted by gelding knife, where men are stoned,
And limbs lopped, and a piteous whimper heard
From spines impaled in dust. Such festivals
Are your delight and fill heaven with loathing.
So your whole shape and semblance testifies.
A den of lions lapping gore were fit
To entertain you, not this opulent seat
Of prophecy to bear so vile a taint.
Hence, loathsome creatures, hence unshepherded,
A herd for whom there is no love in heaven!

CHORUS: O Lord Apollo, hear us in our turn.
Thou art not an abettor in this work;
Thou art the doer, on thee lies the whole guilt.

APOLLO: How might that be? Prolong thy speech so far.

CHORUS: He slew his mother obedient to thy word.

APOLLO: My word commanded vengeance for his father.

CHORUS: So promising acceptance of fresh blood.

APOLLO: And for it absolution at this house.

CHORUS: Would you insult the band which drove him hither?

APOLLO: My mansion is not fit for such as you.

CHORUS: And yet this is the task appointed us.

APOLLO: What is this power and boasted privilege?

CHORUS: We drive the mother-murderer from home.

APOLLO: What of the woman then who slew her man?

CHORUS: That is not death by kin and common blood.

APOLLO: Dishonoured then and set at naught by thee
The marriage-bond which Zeus and Hera seal,
Dishonoured too the Cyprian, from whom
Mankind receive their nearest, dearest joys.
What bond is stronger than the bed of man
And wife, which Fate conjoins and Justice guards?
If then on those who slay their dearest thou
Dost not look down in wrath nor punish them,
Then I declare it is unjust in thee
To persecute Orestes—here I see
Anger, there quietness. But in this suit
The goddess Pallas shall regard and judge.

CHORUS: Him will I never leave nor let him go.

APOLLO: Pursue him then, pile up more labour lost.

CHORUS: No words of thine shall circumscribe my powers.

APOLLO: I would disdain such powers at a gift.

CHORUS: Ay, *thou* art called great at the throne of Zeus.
But I—a mother's blood is calling me
To seek revenge and follow up the hunt.

APOLLO: And I will help and guard my suppliant.
A fearful thing in heaven and on earth
Would be the wrath of such, if I broke faith.

(Interval of one year. Before a shrine of Athena in Athens: enter Orestes)

ORESTES: O Queen Athena, at Loxias' command
I come to thee; receive me mercifully;
An outcast, yet no more with sullied hands,
The edge of my pollution worn away
At distant homes of men, on weary paths
By land and sea alike, obedient
To the prophetic word of Loxias,

Present before thy image, entering
Thy house, O Goddess, here with constant heart
I wait the consummation of my cause.
(Enter the Chorus)

CHORUS: Aha! here are his traces plain to see.
Step where our dumb informer points the way;
For as the hound pursues the wounded fawn,
So follow I the smell of dripping blood.
With toil and sweat of many a weary day
My bosom pants; all the wide earth I roamed,
And traversing the sea in wingless flight,
Close in his vessel's wake, I follow still.
He must be crouching somewhere here—I feel
My senses wooed with smell of human blood.

—Beware, again beware!
Look on all sides, for fear
He find some escape, foul mother-murderer.

—Ah, here he is, craving help,
As in a close embrace he clasps that divine
Image, awaiting trial for his handiwork.

—It cannot be! The mother's blood he shed
Can ne'er be raised up again.
Low on the ground it lies, scattered away and lost.

—Soon from thy living flesh shalt thou repay
Offerings rich and red; and on an evil draught
From thee my lips shall feed in fat pasturage.

—Alive and wasted, I shall drag thee down
To pay the full price of that terrible act of blood,

—And others shalt thou see in hell who did
Evil to strangers, Gods,
Or unto those dearest that gave them life,
Each well requited with his just reward.

—For Hades is a stern inquisitor
Of mankind below;
All things are written down in that watchful heart.

ORESTES: Taught in the school of suffering, I have learnt
The times and seasons when it is right to keep
Silence and when to break it; and in this matter
A wise instructor has charged me to speak.
The blood upon my hands has sunk to sleep,
The matricidal stain is washed away.
Still fresh it was when at the hearth divine
Of Phoebus it was purged by sacrifice.
Too many to recount the men who have
Received since then my presence without hurt;
And now with lips made pure and reverent
I call to my defence this country's Queen,
Athena, who with bloodless victory
Shall win me and my people to her side
In true alliance for all time to come.
So, whether on far shores of Libya,
By Trito's waters, where she came to birth,
Her foot be planted, covered or erect,
Defending those that love her, or her eyes,
Like some brave captain's, watch on Phlegra's heights,
O may she come—far off, she still can hear—
And from these miseries deliver me!

CHORUS: Neither Apollo nor Athena's power
Shall save thee from perdition, when, by all
Abandoned and forsaken, knowing not
Where in the bosom joy resides, shalt thou,
A bloodless shadow, make a feast for fiends.
Hast thou no answer, dost thou spurn me so,
Fattened for me, my consecrated host?
Not slain upon the altar, nay alive
Thou shalt feed me, and now shalt hear a chant
Which binds thee fast unto my purposes.

FIRST STASIMON

O come, let us dance in a ring and declare,
As our purpose is fixed,
To the tune of this terrible music
Those laws whereby
We determine the fortune of mortals.
Just, we avow, are our judgments and righteous.
All those who can show hands cleanly and pure,
Unharmed shall they live for the length of their days,
No anger of ours shall afflict them;
But the man, like him, who hath sinned and conceals
Hands dripping with blood shall be summoned
To attest for the slaughtered the truth of their cause
And to pay for their blood retribution.

STR. I

Mother Night, thy children cry, hear, black Night,
As we deal to man in dark and day fell judgment!
The son born of Leto hath plundered my powers,
Stealing that trembling hare, held a due sacrifice
Mother's blood to expiate.
  Over the blood now to be shed madness and moil,
  Wither and waste, melody dismal and deathly.
  Hymn of hell to harp untuned,
  Chant to bind the soul in chains,
  Spell to parch the flesh to dust.

ANT. I

This the Fates who move the whole world through, charged
Unto us to be our task for all time hence,
Watch to keep over all hands that drip red with kindred
Blood, to wait till the Earth open—then down in hell
Freedom hardly shall they find.
  Over the blood now to be shed madness and moil,
  Wither and waste, melody dismal and deathly.
  Hymn of hell to harp untuned,
  Chant to bind the soul in chains,
  Spell to parch the flesh to dust.

STR. 2

Such were the powers decreed as we came into being,
Only to touch not immortals, and none of Olympus
Seeketh a share in our banquets.
Part have we none in the raiment of white, for in such
we delight not;
Other pleasures are our choice—
Wreck of the house, when at the hearth
Blood of its own drippeth in strife.
Hard on his heels ever we run, and tho' his strength be great,
Lured by fresh blood we waste and wear him out.

ANT. 2

Yet, as we seek to relieve other Gods of this office
And by our own intent endeavour exempt them
So that none call them to question,
Zeus doth debar this brood, bloodstained and abhorrent,
from converse,
Yea, disdains our company.
Wreck of the house, when at the hearth
Blood of its own drippeth in strife.
Hard on his heels ever we run, and tho' his strength be great,
Lured by fresh blood we waste and wear him out.

STR. 3

Glories of men, how great in the day is their grandeur!
Yet shall they fade in the darkness of hell in dishonour,
Faced with our raiment of sable and dancing
Feet well-tuned to melodies malign.
Nimbly my feet leap and descend,
High in the air, down to the earth,
Heavy the tread of my tiptoe,
Fugitive steps suddenly tripped up in fatal confusion.

ANT. 3

Caught unawares doth he stumble, his wickedness blinds him,
Such is the cloud of pollution that hovers around him.

Thick on the house is the darkness, a story
Which mankind shall tell with mournful tongue.
  Nimbly my feet leap and descend,
  High in the air, down to the earth,
  Heavy the tread of my tiptoe,
  Fugitive steps suddenly tripped up in fatal confusion.

STR. 4
Our task is such. Armed with quick
Resource and keen memories,
We keep with hard hearts unmoved constant watch on
    human sin.
What all dishonour honour we,
From whence the Gods are barred
By dark corruption foul, region of rugged ways
Both for the quick and dead, for blind and seeing too.

ANT. 4
What mortal then boweth not
In fear and dread, while he hears
The ordinance which Fate made ours, the gift of heaven too,
A perfect power and privilege
Of ancient ages? We
Are not unhonoured, tho' deep in the earth the clime
Set for us, sunk in sunless, everlasting gloom.
(Enter Athena)

ATHENA: I heard a cry far off, calling to me,
Where by Scamander's waters I received
Possession of the lands which have been given
By the Achaean princes for my own
To have and hold for ever, a chosen gift
To grace the sons of Theseus. Thence I came
In fleet pursuit of never-wearied foot,
With wingless beat of this deep-bosomed aegis—
To such a car my lusty steeds were yoked.
And now, regarding this strange company,

I have no fear, yet wonder fills my eyes.
Who can you be? To all I speak in common,
Both to this stranger seated at my image,
And you, resembling no begotten seed,
Neither like goddesses beheld in heaven
Nor fashioned in the figure of mankind.
But to speak harm of others without cause
Would ill accord with justice and with right.

CHORUS: Daughter of Zeus, in brief thou shalt learn all.
We are the dismal daughters of dark Night,
Called Curses in the palaces of hell.

ATHENA: Your names I know then and your origin.

CHORUS: And now we will acquaint you with our powers.

ATHENA: Teach me those also; I am fain to learn.

CHORUS: We drive the homicide from hearth and home.

ATHENA: And tell me where his persecution ends.

CHORUS: Where to be joyful is a thing unknown.

ATHENA: Is that your hue and cry against this man?

CHORUS: It is; for he thought fit to kill his mother.

ATHENA: He feared, perhaps, some other grave displeasure?

CHORUS: What could have driven him to matricide?

ATHENA: Two parties are there and but half the cause.

CHORUS: Our oath he will not take, nor give his own.

ATHENA: You seek the name of justice, not the act.

CHORUS: How so? Instruct, since thou hast wealth of wit.

ATHENA: Seek not by oaths to make the wrong prevail.

CHORUS: Then try the case and give us a straight judgment.

ATHENA: Will you commit the verdict to my charge?

CHORUS: I will, since thou art worthy, and thy sire.

ATHENA: Stranger, what is thy answer? Let us know
Thy fatherland and family, and what
Misfortune overtook thee, and then meet
The charge they bring against thee. If with trust
In justice thou art stationed at my image,
A holy suppliant, as Ixion was,
Then render on each count a clear reply.

ORESTES: O Queen Athena, those last words of thine
Shall be my preface to relieve thy care.
No suppliant I that would be purified.
With hands already spotless I embraced
Thy image and took session at thy shrine;
And I can give thee evidence. The law
Commands the manslayer to hold his peace
Till he has been anointed with the blood
Of new-born beast by purifying hands.
Long since at other houses and on paths
Of land and sea have I been thus absolved.
So, having cast this scruple from thy mind,
I will inform thee of my origin.
I am from Argos, and my father's name—
For asking that I thank thee—Agamemnon,
Marshal of men in ships, with whom of late
The city of Ilium thou hast made to be
No more a city. He died an evil death.
When he returned home, my black-hearted mother
Killed him, entrapped in cunningly contrived
Nets that bore witness to a bath of blood.
Therefore, when I returned from banishment,
I killed my mother—that I do confess—
In retribution for my father's death:
An act not wholly mine, for Loxias
Must answer for it too, who spoke to me
Of bitter anguish to afflict my spirit

If I should fail in vengeance on the guilty.
Whether 'twas just or no, be thou my judge.
I will accept thy ordering of my doom.

ATHENA: Too grave a suit is this for mortal minds
To judge, nor is it right that such as I
Should pass my verdict on a suit of blood
Shed with such bitter wrath attending it;
And all the more since thou hast come to me
A suppliant pure and humbled; and also I
Respect thee, being innocent of wrong
Against my city. But no such gentleness
Has been appointed *these*, and if their plea
Fall short of victory, the poison which
Drips from their angry bosoms to the ground
Will lay this country waste with pestilence.
So stands the matter—let them stay or be
Dismissed, the issue is fraught with injury.
But be it so; since it is come to this,
Judges I will appoint for homicide,
A court set up in perpetuity.
Meanwhile do you call proofs and witnesses
As sworn supports of justice; then, having chosen
The best of all my people, I shall come
To pass true judgment on the present cause.
(Exit Athena)

STR. I SECOND STASIMON

Now shall ancient ordinance
Fall to naught, should the unjust appeal of that accurst
Matricide win the day.
Now shall all men be reconciled by that
Crime to acts of violence;
Many, many a pain awaiteth
Parents in the time to come,
Struck by true-begotten child.

ANT. 1

We who watch the works of men
Shall not send wrath to haunt evildoers, rather lend
Rein to all deeds of blood.
Then shall one, making known his neighbour's plight,
From another seek to learn
End or easement of his trouble—
Wretch, what shifting remedies
Shall he recommend in vain!

STR. 2

Then let none, if e'er he fall
Smitten by disaster, cry
Out in lamentation, 'Oh
Justice, O Furies, hearken to my prayer!'—
Thus shall fathers groan and thus
Stricken mothers weep in vain;
Since the house of Righteousness
Falls in ruins to the ground.

ANT. 2

Times there be when fear is well;
Yea, it must continually
Watch within the soul enthroned.
Needful too straits to teach humility.
Who of those that never nursed
Healthy dread within the heart,
Be they men or peoples, shall
Show to Justice reverence?

STR. 3

Choose a life despot-free,
Yet restrained by rule of law. Thus and thus
God doth administer, yet he appointeth the mean as
the master in all things.
Hear my word proportionate:
Wickedness breedeth, and pride is the name of her child,

While from the spirit
Of health is born blessedness
Prayed for and prized of all men.

ANT. 3
So in brief this I say,
Bow before the shrine of Right, neither be
Tempted by profit to spurn it with insolent feet;
retribution shall follow.
Yet abides the end decreed.
See that thy father and mother are rightly esteemed;
Grant to the stranger
Within thy gates all the due
Honours of entertainment.

STR. 4
The man who seeks what is right
Of choice and free will, shall not be unblest;
The seed of just men shall never perish.
Not so the froward | and foolish heart that bears
A motley cargo of iniquity.
His outspread sail shall soon be hauled down;
Caught in the growing storm his stout
Mast shall be rent and shattered.

ANT. 4
To ears that hear not he cries,
To angry seas which he cannot master;
His guardian spirit | doth laugh to see him,
Who rashly boasted | his ship would come to port,
So weak and faint he cannot breast the wave
And sinks unseen with all his riches,
Dashed on the reef of Justice, un-
Looked-on and unlamented.

(Enter Athena with the Judges, followed by citizens of Athens)

ATHENA: Herald, proclaim, hold back the multitude,
Then let the trump Tyrrhenian, filled with breath

Of human lips, raise its resounding cry!
For while this great tribunal is enrolled,
Silence is meet and study of my laws
For this whole city now and evermore,
And likewise for these litigants, and so
Just judgment shall be given on their cause.

(Enter Apollo)

CHORUS: O Lord Apollo, rule where power is thine.
What business is there that concerns thee here?

APOLLO: I come both as a witness, the accused
Being a suppliant at my sanctuary
And purified of bloodshed at my hands,
And also to be tried with him, for I
Must answer for his mother's death. Do thou
Open the case and judge as thou knowest how.

ATHENA: The case is open. Yours it is to speak.
The prosecutor shall take precedence
And so instruct us truly what befell.

CHORUS: Many in number, we shall be brief in speech.
Give answer to our questions one by one.
First, is it true that thou didst kill thy mother?

ORESTES: I killed her. That is true, and not denied.

CHORUS: So then the first of the three rounds is ours.

ORESTES: You need not boast that you have thrown me yet.

CHORUS: But, having killed her, thou must tell us how.

ORESTES: I will. With drawn sword levelled at the throat.

CHORUS: Who moved, who counselled thee to such an act?

ORESTES: The oracle of the God who is my witness.

CHORUS: The Prophet taught thee to do matricide!

ORESTES: And I have not repented to this day.

CHORUS: Condemned anon, thou shalt tell another tale.

ORESTES: My father shall defend me from the grave.

CHORUS: Ah, having slain thy mother, trust the dead!

ORESTES: She was polluted with a double crime.

CHORUS: How so? Expound thy meaning to the court.

ORESTES: She slew her husband, and she slew my father.

CHORUS: Well, she died guiltless, thou art still alive.

ORESTES: Why, when she lived, did you not harass *her*?

CHORUS: She was not bound by blood to him she slew.

ORESTES: And am I then in blood bound to my mother?

CHORUS: How did she nourish thee, abandoned wretch,
Within the womb? Dost thou abjure the tie,
Nearest and dearest, of a mother's blood?

ORESTES: Do *thou* declare thy witness now; pronounce,
Apollo, whether I was justified.
I killed as I have said; that is confessed;
But in thy judgment was it justly done?

APOLLO: Athena's great tribunal, I will say,
Justly; and I, as prophet, cannot lie.
Never upon my throne of prophecy
Have I spoke aught of people, man or woman
But what my father Zeus commanded me.
How strong that justice is instruct yourselves
And do according to my father's will,
Whose sovranty no oath shall override.

CHORUS: Zeus, as thou sayest, gave thee this command,
To charge Orestes to avenge his father
Regardless of dishonouring his mother?

APOLLO: 'Tis not the same, to kill a noble man
Invested with all majesty from heaven,
A woman too to kill him, and not with far
Shafts of a valiant Amazon's archery,
But in such manner as you shall be told,
Thou, Pallas, and this bench of justicers
Appointed to give judgment on this cause.
When he returned from battle, bringing home
A balance for the greater part of good,
At first she welcomed him with gentle words,
And then, attending while he bathed, at last,
His head pavilioned in a trailing robe,
She struck him, fettered in those opulent folds.
Such was his end—a man, a king whom all
The world had honoured, a mighty admiral,
And such the woman who contrived his death
As I have told, seeking to move the hearts
Of all who are assembled here to judge.

CHORUS: Then Zeus gives precedence to the father's death
According to thy plea. Yet Zeus it was
Who bound in chains his aged father Kronos.
How shall thy plea be reconciled with that?
Judges, I call upon you to take note.

APOLLO: Abominable monsters loathed of heaven,
Chains may be loosened, there are cures for that
And many a means to bring deliverance;
But once the dust has drunk a dead man's blood,
He shall not rise again—for that no charm
My father has appointed, though all else
He turns and overturns and sets in place
Without the endeavour of a laboured breath.

CHORUS: See what this plea for the acquittal means.
He spilt upon the ground his mother's blood,
And shall he still dwell in his father's house?

What altars of the people shall he use,
What holy water grant him fellowship?

APOLLO: That too will I declare, and mark the truth.
The mother is not the parent of the child,
Only the nurse of what she has conceived.
The parent is the father, who commits
His seed to her, a stranger, to be held
With God's help in safe keeping. In proof of this,
Father there might be and no mother: see
A witness here, child of Olympian Zeus,
Begotten not in wedlock neither bred
In darkness of the womb, a goddess whom
No other goddess could have brought to birth.
And therefore, Pallas, since in all things I
Shall strive to make thy land and people great,
I sent this man to be thy suppliant,
A faithful friend to thee eternally,
That thou, Goddess, might find a staunch ally
In him and his hereafter, a covenant
For this thy people to uphold for ever.

ATHENA: Enough has now been spoken. Therefore shall I
Command the judges to record their votes
In righteous judgment according to their minds?

APOLLO: Empty our quiver, every arrow spent.
We wait to hear the issue of the trial.

ATHENA: How shall my ruling be approved by you?

CHORUS: Sirs, you have heard, and vote accordingly
With hearty reverence for your solemn oath.

ATHENA: People of Athens, hear my ordinance
At this first trial for bloodshed. Evermore
This great tribunal shall abide in power
Among the sons of Aegeus; and this hill
Whereon of old the Amazons encamped,

When hate of Theseus rallied them to arms,
And here a city newly-fortified
Upraised against his own, and sacrificed
To Ares, whereupon this rock was named
The Areopagus—here Reverence
And inbred Fear enthroned among my people
Shall hold their hands from evil night and day,
Only let them not tamper with their laws;
For, should a stream of mire pollute the pure
Fountain, the lips shall never find it sweet.
I bid my people honour and uphold
The mean between the despot and the slave,
And not to banish terror utterly,
For what man shall be upright without fear?
And if you honour this high ordinance,
Then shall you have for land and commonweal
A stronghold of salvation, such as none
Hath elsewhere in the world, in Scythia
Nor in the isle of Pelops. I establish
This great tribunal to protect my people,
Grave, quick to anger, incorruptible,
And ever vigilant over those that sleep.
Such is my exhortation unto all
My people for all generations. Now
Arise, take each his ballot, and upon
Your solemn oath give judgment. I have spoken.

CHORUS: Remember us, I charge you, visitants
Grave in displeasure, and respect our powers.

APOLLO: I charge you to respect the oracles
Ordained of Zeus and see that they bear fruit.

CHORUS: Bloodshed is not thy office, and henceforth
The shrines which voice thy utterance are unholy.

APOLLO: Then did my Father err when he resolved
To cleanse Ixion, the first murderer?

CHORUS: Prate on; but, if my cause should fail, I shall
Afflict this people with a heavy hand.

APOLLO: Thou art unhonoured of all deities
Both young and old, and victory shall be mine.

CHORUS: In the house of Pheres once thou didst the like,
Tempting the Fates to make a man immortal.

APOLLO: Is it not just at all times to befriend
A worshipper, and most in time of need?

CHORUS: Thou didst destroy the ancient dispensations,
Beguiling antique deities with wine.

APOLLO: Thou, failing of the verdict presently,
Shalt spew thy poisons, but they shall do no harm.

CHORUS: Thy youth has trampled on my honoured age.
Therefore I wait the verdict, whether or no
Upon this city to let loose my rage.

ATHENA: The final judgment is a task for me;
So for Orestes shall this vote be cast.
No mother gave me birth, and in all things
Save marriage I, my father's child indeed,
With all my heart commend the masculine.
Wherefore I shall not hold of higher worth
A woman who was killed because she killed
Her wedded lord and master of her home.
Upon an equal vote Orestes wins.
Let the appointed judges now proceed
To count the ballots from the emptied urn.

ORESTES: O bright Apollo, how shall the judgment go?

CHORUS: O mother mine, black Night, dost thou behold?

ORESTES: My hour has come—the halter or the light.

CHORUS: And mine—to keep my ancient powers, or perish.

APOLLO: Sirs, count the issue of the votes aright;
Divide them as you honour what is just.
If judgment fail, great harm shall come of it;
And oft one vote hath raised a fallen house.

ATHENA: He stands acquitted on the charge of blood.
The number of the counted votes is equal.

ORESTES: O Pallas, O deliverer of my house,
I was an outcast from my country, thou
Hast brought me home again; and men shall say,
Once more he is an Argive and he dwells
In his paternal heritage by the grace
Of Pallas, and of Loxias, and third
Of him who orders all, Deliverer,
Who had regard unto my father's death
And has delivered me. Before I go
I pledge my honour to this land of thine
And to thy people for all plenitude
Of after generations that no prince
Of Argos shall lead forth his serried arms
In war against this city. We ourselves
Out of the grave which then shall cover us
Shall so afflict all those who would transgress
The pledge that I have given, with desperate
Obstructions, wanderings disconsolate
And adverse omens frowning on their march,
That they shall soon repent; but if they keep
Our covenant, continuing to honour
Athena's city with arms confederate,
With blessings rather shall we visit them.
And so farewell. May thou and those who rule
Thy populace stand firm in such a stance
As shall prevail against all enemies,
A strong salvation and victory at arms! *(Exit)*

KOMMOS

CHORUS: Oho ye younger Gods, since ye have trod under foot
The laws of old and ancient powers purloined,
Then we, dishonoured, deadly in displeasure,
Shall spread poison foul
Through the land, with damp contagion
Of rage malignant, bleak and barren, blasting, withering up the earth,
Mildews on bud and birth abortive. Oh!
Venomous pestilence
Shall sweep this country with infectious death.
To weep?—nay, to work; yea, to work ill, to lay low the people!
Oh me, many the wrongs of these maids of Night
Mourning their plundered honours!

ATHENA: Let me persuade you from this passionate grief.
You are not vanquished; the issue of the trial
Has been determined by an equal vote.
Nay, Zeus it was who plainly testified,
Himself pronouncing his own evidence,
That for this deed Orestes should not suffer.
And therefore be not angry, let no dread
Displeasures fall upon this country, nor
Corrupt her fruits with drops of rank decay
And keen-edged cankers in the early bud.
Rather accept my honourable word
That ye shall have a cave wherein to dwell
Among this righteous people, and, enthroned
In honour at your altars, shall receive
The adoration of my citizens.

CHORUS: Oho ye younger Gods, since ye have trod under foot
The laws of old and ancient powers purloined,
Then we, dishonoured, deadly in displeasure,
Shall spread poison foul
Through the land, with damp contagion

Of rage malignant, bleak and barren, blasting, withering up
the earth,
Mildews on bud and birth abortive. Oh!
Venomous pestilence
Shall sweep this country with infectious death.
To weep?—nay, to work; yea, to work ill, to lay low the people!
Oh me, many the wrongs of these maids of Night
Mourning their plundered honours!

ATHENA: Nay, *not* dishonoured; neither let divine
Displeasures plague this mortal populace.
I too confide in Zeus—why speak of that?
And I alone of all divinities
Know of the keys which guard the treasury
Of heaven's thunder. Of that there is no need:
Be moved by my persuasion not to bring
From angry tongues to birth a fruit accursed
Nor sweep this country with calamities.
Calm the black humours of embittered rage,
Reside with me, and share my majesty;
And when from these wide acres you enjoy
Year after year the harvest offerings
That wedlock may be blest with issue, then
You will commend me for my intercession.

CHORUS: Me to be treated so!
Me with the sage wisdom of years to dwell here, oh
Ever debased, oh defiled!
Spirit of spleen and unyielding spite!
Give ear, O Earth!
Ah, the insufferable pangs sink deep.
Hear my passion, hear, black Night!
For the powers once mine, sealed long, long ago,
Have by the younger Gods been snatched all away.

ATHENA: My elder art thou, therefore I indulge
Thy passion; yet, though not so wise as thou,

To me also hath Zeus vouchsafed the gift
Of no mean understanding. I declare,
If you depart from this to other lands,
This country yet shall prove your heart's desire;
For with the tide of years shall flow increase
Of honour to my people; wherefore thou,
Honoured among them and enthroned hard by
The temple of Erechtheus, shalt receive
Such homage from the congregated throngs
Of men and women as shall ne'er be yours
Elsewhere in all the world. And so, I pray,
Lay not upon my territories the spur
Of internecine strife to prick the breast
Of manhood flown with passion as with wine;
Implant not in my sons the bravery
Of fighting-cocks, embroiled against their own.
Abroad let battle rage for every heart
Possessed by love of glory—that shall be theirs
In plenty. This then is my offer to you—
To give and take rich benefits and share
My honours in a land beloved of heaven.

CHORUS: Me to be treated so!
Me with the sage wisdom of years to dwell here, oh
Ever debased, oh defiled!
Spirit of spleen and unyielding spite!
Give ear, O Earth!
Ah, the insufferable pangs sink deep.
Hear my passion, hear, black Night!
For the powers once mine, sealed long, long ago,
Have by the younger Gods been snatched all away.

ATHENA: I will not weary of my benedictions,
Lest it be ever said that thou, so old
A deity, wast driven from the land
By me and by my mortal citizens,
Rejected without welcome and despised.

Nay, if Persuasion's holy majesty,
The sweet enchantment of these lips divine,
Is aught to thee, why then, reside with me;
But if thou wilt not, surely it were wrong
To lay upon my citizens a load
Of indignation and pernicious rage,
Since it is in thy power to own the soil
Justly attended with the highest honours.

CHORUS: O Queen Athena, what dost thou promise me?

ATHENA: A dwelling free of sorrow. Pray, accept.

CHORUS: Say I accept, what honours shall be mine?

ATHENA: No house shall prosper save by grace from thee.

CHORUS: Wilt thou ensure me this prerogative?

ATHENA: I will, and bless all those who worship thee.

CHORUS: And pledge a warrant for all time to come?

ATHENA: I need not promise what I would not do.

CHORUS: Thy charms are working, and my rage subsides.

ATHENA: Here make thy dwelling where thou shalt win friends.

CHORUS: What song then shall I chant over the land?

ATHENA: A song of faultless victory: from earth and sea,
From skies above may gentle breezes blow,
And, breathing sunshine, float from shore to shore;
That corn and cattle may continually
Increase and multiply, and that no harm
Befall the offspring of humanity;
And prosper too the fruit of righteous hearts;
For I, as one who tends flowers in a garden,
Delight in those, the seeds that bring no sorrow.
Such is thy part; and in the glorious
Arrays of battle I shall strive until

This city, over all victorious,
Enjoy an honoured name throughout the world.

STR. I

THIRD STASIMON

CHORUS: I accept. Here with Pallas I will dwell,
Honouring the city which
Zeus Almighty with the aid of Ares
Holds a fortress for the Gods,
Jewelled crown of Greece and guardian of her sanctuaries.
So for her I pray with all
Graciousness of utterance
That smiling sun and bounteous earth unite to yield
Lifelong joys, fortunes fair,
Light and Darkness reconciled.

ATHENA: As a favour to all of my people have I
Given homes in the land unto these, whose power
Is so great and their anger so hard to appease—
All that concerneth mankind they dispense.
Yet whenever a man falls foul of their wrath,
He knoweth not whence his afflictions approach;
Apprehended to answer the sins of his sires,
He is led unto these to be judged, and the still
Stroke of perdition
In the dust shall stifle his proud boast.

ANT. I

CHORUS: Ne'er may foul winds be stirred to touch with blight
Budding tree—a grace from me;
Ne'er may parching droughts that blind the newly
Parted blossom trespass here;
Ne'er may blasts of noisome plague advance across the fields;
Rather, Pan in season due
Grant that flocks and herds may yield
A twin increase of yearly wealth, and from the rich
Store which these Gods vouchsafe
May the Earth repay them well.

ATHENA: O listen, ye guards of my city, and hear
What blessings they bring you! For great is the power
Of the Furies in heaven and hell, and on earth
Unto some glad music, to others again
They dispense days darkened with weeping.

STR. 2

CHORUS: Sudden death cutting short
Manhood's prime I bid away;
To all her comely daughters grant
Husband and home, O heavenly wardens of wedlock,
And ye too, dread Fates, born of the same mother's womb,
Spirits of justice divine, dwelling in every household,
Present at every season, weighty in your majesty,
Praised and magnified in every place.

ATHENA: Fair blessings are these they bestow on the land,
And my heart is rejoiced.
To the eye of Persuasion I give all praise,
That with favour she looked on the breath of my lips
As I strove to appease these powers that once
Were averted in anger; but Zeus who is Lord
Of the eloquent word hath prevailed, and at last
In contention for blessings we conquer.

ANT. 2

CHORUS: Ne'er, I pray, ne'er may that
Root of evil, civil strife,
Rage within her boundaries;
Ne'er may the earth's dust drink of the blood of her children,
And wroth thereat thirst greedily after revenge,
Blood in requital of blood;
Rather in friendly communion
Gladness be rendered for gladness,
All at one in love and hate.
Therein lies a cure for human ills.

ATHENA: How quick is their sense to discover the paths
Of a tongue fair-spoken! From these dread shapes
Great gain do I see for my people: if ye
Pay homage to these and with favour regard
Their favour to you, then surely the fame
Of a city in justice and equity ruled
Shall be spread as a light unto all men.
(Enter Escort of Women, carrying crimson robes and torches)

STR. 3
CHORUS: Joy to you, joy of your justly appointed riches,
Joy to all the people, blest
With the Virgin's love, who sits
Next beside her Father's throne.
Wisdom ye have learned at last.
Folded under Pallas' wing,
Yours at last the grace of Zeus.

ATHENA: Joy to you likewise! Walking before you,
To the chambers appointed I show you the way,
Led by the sacred lights of the escort.
Come with me, come, and let solemn oblations
Speed you in joy to your homes in the earth,
Where all that is hurtful imprison, we pray,
And release what shall guide them to glory.
Lead them, O daughters of Cranaus, lead them,
And let all of you bear
Good will for the good that is given.

ANT. 3
CHORUS: Joy to you, joy—yet again we pronounce our blessing—
Joy to all the citizens,
Mortals, deities alike.
While you hold this land and pay
Homage to our residence,
Ne'er shall you have cause to blame
Change and chance in human life.

ATHENA: I thank you for these words of benison,
And now with flames of torchlit splendour bright
Escort you to your subterranean home,
Attended by the wardens of my shrine,
And justly so; for meet it is that all
The eye of Theseus' people should come forth,
This noble company of maidens fair,
And women wed and venerable in years.
Adorn them well in robes of crimson dye,
And let these blazing torches lead the way,
So that the good will of these residents
Be proved in manly prowess of your sons.

(The Chorus has put on the crimson robes; and a procession is drawn up, led by twenty-four young men, who are followed by the Chorus and their escort, and the main body of the citizens. The rest is sung as the procession moves away)

STR. I — CHORUS OF THE ESCORT

Pass on your way, O ye powers majestic,
Daughters of darkness, in happy procession.
Hush, O people, and speak all fair!

ANT. I

Pass to the caverns of earth immemorial
There to be worshipped in honour and glory.
Hush, O people, and speak all fair!

STR. 2

Gracious and kindly of heart to our people,
Hither, O holy ones, hither in gladness,
Follow the lamps that illumine the way.
O sing at the end Alleluia!

ANT. 2

Peace to you, peace of a happy communion,
People of Pallas. Zeus who beholdeth
All with the Fates is at last reconciled.
O sing at the end Alleluia!

ABOUT THE INTRODUCER

RICHARD SEAFORD has been Professor of Ancient Greek Literature at the University of Exeter since 1995. His publications include *Euripides: Cyclops*; *Reciprocity and Ritual: Homer and Tragedy in the Developing City-State*; *Euripides: Bacchae* and *Money and the Early Greek Mind.* He has been a member of the National Humanities Center (North Carolina) and Distinguished Visiting Professor at the University of Texas at Austin.

ABOUT THE TRANSLATOR

GEORGE THOMSON was a Fellow of King's College, Cambridge, and afterwards Professor of Greek at the University of Birmingham from 1937 to 1970. His numerous publications include *Aeschylus and Athens*, *Studies in Ancient Greek Society* (2 vols) and *The Human Essence.* His last book, about the lost culture of the Blasket Islands, was *Island Home* (1988).

TITLES IN EVERYMAN'S LIBRARY

CHINUA ACHEBE
Things Fall Apart

AESCHYLUS
The Oresteia

THE ARABIAN NIGHTS
(2 vols, tr. Husain Haddawy)

AUGUSTINE
The Confessions

JANE AUSTEN
Emma
Mansfield Park
Northanger Abbey
Persuasion
Pride and Prejudice
Sanditon and Other Stories
Sense and Sensibility

HONORÉ DE BALZAC
Cousin Bette
Eugénie Grandet
Old Goriot

SIMONE DE BEAUVOIR
The Second Sex

SAMUEL BECKETT
Molloy, Malone Dies,
The Unnamable
(US only)

SAUL BELLOW
The Adventures of Augie March

HECTOR BERLIOZ
The Memoirs of Hector Berlioz

WILLIAM BLAKE
Poems and Prophecies

JORGE LUIS BORGES
Ficciones

JAMES BOSWELL
The Life of Samuel Johnson
The Journal of a Tour to
the Hebrides

CHARLOTTE BRONTË
Jane Eyre
Villette

EMILY BRONTË
Wuthering Heights

MIKHAIL BULGAKOV
The Master and Margarita

SAMUEL BUTLER
The Way of all Flesh

JAMES M. CAIN
The Postman Always Rings Twice
Double Indemnity
Mildred Pierce
Selected Stories
(1 vol. US only)

ITALO CALVINO
If on a winter's night a traveler

ALBERT CAMUS
The Outsider (UK)
The Stranger (US)

WILLA CATHER
Death Comes for the Archbishop
My Ántonia
(US only)

MIGUEL DE CERVANTES
Don Quixote

RAYMOND CHANDLER
The novels (2 vols)
Collected Stories

GEOFFREY CHAUCER
Canterbury Tales

ANTON CHEKHOV
My Life and Other Stories
The Steppe and Other Stories

KATE CHOPIN
The Awakening

CARL VON CLAUSEWITZ
On War

S. T. COLERIDGE
Poems

WILKIE COLLINS
The Moonstone
The Woman in White

CONFUCIUS
The Analects

JOSEPH CONRAD
Heart of Darkness
Lord Jim
Nostromo
The Secret Agent
Typhoon and Other Stories
Under Western Eyes
Victory

THOMAS CRANMER
The Book of Common Prayer
(UK only)

DANTE ALIGHIERI
The Divine Comedy

CHARLES DARWIN
The Origin of Species
The Voyage of the Beagle
(in 1 vol.)

DANIEL DEFOE
Moll Flanders
Robinson Crusoe

CHARLES DICKENS
Bleak House
David Copperfield
Dombey and Son
Great Expectations
Hard Times
Little Dorrit
Martin Chuzzlewit
Nicholas Nickleby
The Old Curiosity Shop
Oliver Twist
Our Mutual Friend
The Pickwick Papers
A Tale of Two Cities

DENIS DIDEROT
Memoirs of a Nun

JOHN DONNE
The Complete English Poems

FYODOR DOSTOEVSKY
The Adolescent
The Brothers Karamazov
Crime and Punishment
Demons
The Idiot
Notes from Underground

W. E. B. DU BOIS
The Souls of Black Folk
(US only)

GEORGE ELIOT
Adam Bede
Daniel Deronda
Middlemarch
The Mill on the Floss
Silas Marner

WILLIAM FAULKNER
The Sound and the Fury
(UK only)

HENRY FIELDING
Joseph Andrews and Shamela
(UK only)
Tom Jones

F. SCOTT FITZGERALD
The Great Gatsby
This Side of Paradise
(UK only)

PENELOPE FITZGERALD
The Bookshop
The Gate of Angels
The Blue Flower
(in 1 vol.)
Offshore
Human Voices
The Beginning of Spring
(in 1 vol.)

GUSTAVE FLAUBERT
Madame Bovary

FORD MADOX FORD
The Good Soldier
Parade's End

E. M. FORSTER
Howards End
A Passage to India

ELIZABETH GASKELL
Mary Barton

EDWARD GIBBON
The Decline and Fall of the
Roman Empire
Vols 1 to 3: The Western Empire
Vols 4 to 6: The Eastern Empire

J. W. VON GOETHE
Selected Works

IVAN GONCHAROV
Oblomov

GÜNTER GRASS
The Tin Drum

GRAHAM GREENE
Brighton Rock
The Human Factor

DASHIELL HAMMETT
The Maltese Falcon
The Thin Man
Red Harvest
(in 1 vol.)

THOMAS HARDY
Far From the Madding Crowd
Jude the Obscure
The Mayor of Casterbridge
The Return of the Native
Tess of the d'Urbervilles
The Woodlanders

JAROSLAV HAŠEK
The Good Soldier Švejk

NATHANIEL HAWTHORNE
The Scarlet Letter

JOSEPH HELLER
Catch-22

ERNEST HEMINGWAY
A Farewell to Arms
The Collected Stories
(UK only)

GEORGE HERBERT
The Complete English Works

HERODOTUS
The Histories

PATRICIA HIGHSMITH
The Talented Mr. Ripley
Ripley Under Ground
Ripley's Game
(in 1 vol.)

HINDU SCRIPTURES
(tr. R. C. Zaehner)

JAMES HOGG
Confessions of a Justified Sinner

HOMER
The Iliad
The Odyssey

VICTOR HUGO
Les Misérables

HENRY JAMES
The Awkward Age
The Bostonians
The Golden Bowl
The Portrait of a Lady
The Princess Casamassima
The Wings of the Dove
Collected Stories (2 vols)

SAMUEL JOHNSON
A Journey to the Western
Islands of Scotland

JAMES JOYCE
Dubliners
A Portrait of the Artist as
a Young Man
Ulysses

FRANZ KAFKA
Collected Stories
The Castle
The Trial

JOHN KEATS
The Poems

SØREN KIERKEGAARD
Fear and Trembling and
The Book on Adler

RUDYARD KIPLING
Collected Stories
Kim

THE KORAN
(tr. Marmaduke Pickthall)

CHODERLOS DE LACLOS
Les Liaisons dangereuses

GIUSEPPE TOMASI DI
LAMPEDUSA
The Leopard

WILLIAM LANGLAND
Piers Plowman
with (anon.) Sir Gawain and the
Green Knight, Pearl, Sir Orfeo
(UK only)

D. H. LAWRENCE
Collected Stories
The Rainbow
Sons and Lovers
Women in Love

MIKHAIL LERMONTOV
A Hero of Our Time

PRIMO LEVI
If This is a Man and The Truce
(UK only)
The Periodic Table

THE MABINOGION

NICCOLÒ MACHIAVELLI
The Prince

NAGUIB MAHFOUZ
The Cairo Trilogy

THOMAS MANN
Buddenbrooks
Collected Stories (UK only)
Death in Venice and Other Stories
(US only)
Doctor Faustus

KATHERINE MANSFIELD
The Garden Party and Other
Stories

MARCUS AURELIUS
Meditations

GABRIEL GARCÍA MÁRQUEZ
Love in the Time of Cholera
One Hundred Years of Solitude

ANDREW MARVELL
The Complete Poems

CORMAC McCARTHY
The Border Trilogy (US only)

HERMAN MELVILLE
The Complete Shorter Fiction
Moby-Dick

JOHN STUART MILL
On Liberty and Utilitarianism

JOHN MILTON
The Complete English Poems

YUKIO MISHIMA
The Temple of the
Golden Pavilion

MARY WORTLEY MONTAGU
Letters

MICHEL DE MONTAIGNE
The Complete Works

THOMAS MORE
Utopia

TONI MORRISON
Song of Solomon

MURASAKI SHIKIBU
The Tale of Genji

VLADIMIR NABOKOV
Lolita
Pale Fire
Pnin
Speak, Memory

V. S. NAIPAUL
A House for Mr Biswas

THE NEW TESTAMENT
(King James Version)

THE OLD TESTAMENT
(King James Version)

GEORGE ORWELL
Animal Farm
Nineteen Eighty-Four
Essays

THOMAS PAINE
Rights of Man
and Common Sense

BORIS PASTERNAK
Doctor Zhivago

SYLVIA PLATH
The Bell Jar (US only)

PLATO
The Republic
Symposium and Phaedrus

EDGAR ALLAN POE
The Complete Stories

MARCEL PROUST
In Search of Lost Time
(4 vols, UK only)

ALEXANDER PUSHKIN
The Collected Stories

FRANÇOIS RABELAIS
Gargantua and Pantagruel

JOSEPH ROTH
The Radetzky March

JEAN-JACQUES ROUSSEAU
Confessions
The Social Contract and the Discourses

SALMAN RUSHDIE
Midnight's Children

WALTER SCOTT
Rob Roy

WILLIAM SHAKESPEARE
Comedies Vols 1 and 2
Histories Vols 1 and 2
Romances
Sonnets and Narrative Poems
Tragedies Vols 1 and 2

MARY SHELLEY
Frankenstein

ADAM SMITH
The Wealth of Nations

ALEXANDER SOLZHENITSYN
One Day in the Life of Ivan Denisovich

SOPHOCLES
The Theban Plays

MURIEL SPARK
The Prime of Miss Jean Brodie, The Girls of Slender Means, The Driver's Seat, The Only Problem (1 vol.)

CHRISTINA STEAD
The Man Who Loved Children

JOHN STEINBECK
The Grapes of Wrath

STENDHAL
The Charterhouse of Parma
Scarlet and Black

LAURENCE STERNE
Tristram Shandy

ROBERT LOUIS STEVENSON
The Master of Ballantrae and Weir of Hermiston
Dr Jekyll and Mr Hyde and Other Stories

HARRIET BEECHER STOWE
Uncle Tom's Cabin

ITALO SVEVO
Zeno's Conscience

JONATHAN SWIFT
Gulliver's Travels

JUNICHIRŌ TANIZAKI
The Makioka Sisters

W. M. THACKERAY
Vanity Fair

HENRY DAVID THOREAU
Walden

ALEXIS DE TOCQUEVILLE
Democracy in America

LEO TOLSTOY
Collected Shorter Fiction (2 vols)
Anna Karenina
Childhood, Boyhood and Youth
The Cossacks
War and Peace

ANTHONY TROLLOPE
Barchester Towers
Can You Forgive Her?
Doctor Thorne
The Eustace Diamonds
Framley Parsonage
The Last Chronicle of Barset
Phineas Finn
The Small House at Allington
The Warden

IVAN TURGENEV
Fathers and Children
First Love and Other Stories
A Sportsman's Notebook

MARK TWAIN
Tom Sawyer and Huckleberry Finn

JOHN UPDIKE
The Complete Henry Bech (US only)
Rabbit Angstrom

GIORGIO VASARI
Lives of the Painters, Sculptors and Architects

VIRGIL
The Aeneid

VOLTAIRE
Candide and Other Stories

EVELYN WAUGH
The Complete Short Stories
Black Mischief, Scoop, The Loved One, The Ordeal of Gilbert Pinfold (1 vol.)
Brideshead Revisited
Decline and Fall
A Handful of Dust
The Sword of Honour Trilogy
Waugh Abroad: Collected Travel Writing

EDITH WHARTON
The Age of Innocence
The Custom of the Country
The House of Mirth
The Reef

OSCAR WILDE
Plays, Prose Writings and Poems

MARY WOLLSTONECRAFT
A Vindication of the Rights of Woman

VIRGINIA WOOLF
To the Lighthouse
Mrs Dalloway

WILLIAM WORDSWORTH
Selected Poems (UK only)

W. B. YEATS
The Poems (UK only)

ÉMILE ZOLA
Germinal